ELEPHANTS
and IVORY

TRUE TALES OF HUNTING AND ADVENTURE

BY

JOHN ALFRED JORDEN

AS TOLD TO

JOHN PREBBLE

WITH INTRODUCTION BY
MIKE RESNICK, SERIES EDITOR

Old snapshots from John Alfred Jordan's album

From the original edition's dust jacket.

ELEPHANTS and IVORY

TRUE TALES OF HUNTING AND ADVENTURE

BY

JOHN ALFRED JORDEN

AS TOLD TO

JOHN PREBBLE

WITH INTRODUCTION BY

MIKE RESNICK, SERIES EDITOR

THE RESNICK LIBRARY OF AFRICAN ADVENTURE

No. 8 in the series

Publisher: Ralph Roberts
Vice-President/Operations: Pat Roberts

Resnick Library of African Adventure
Series Editor: Mike Resnick

Editor: Ralph Roberts

Cover Design: Ralph Roberts
Interior Design & Electronic Page Assembly: **WorldComm**®
Photographs as indicated

Originally published in 1956, reprinted by permission of the
copyright holder, Mr. John Prebble, author.

10 9 8 7 6 5 4 3 2 1

ISBN 1-57090-183-X trade paper
ISBN 1-57090-184-8 limited edition hardback

Alexander Books—a division of Creativity, Inc.—is a full–service
publisher located at 65 Macedonia Road, Alexander NC 28701. Phone
(828) 252–9515, Fax (828) 255–8719. For orders only: 1-800-472-0438.
Visa and MasterCard accepted.

This book is also available on the internet in the **Publishers CyberMall**.
Set your browser to **http://abooks.com** and enjoy the many fine values
available there.

INTRODUCTION

His name was John Alfred Jordan, and he was one of the great African adventurers in the early days of this century.

That name is almost forgotten today. Certainly it is never mentioned in the same breath as that of Karamojo Bell, or F.C. Selous, or Pondoro Taylor, or Deaf Banks, or Arthur Neumann, or James Sutherland — but there is a reason for it. They were all legitimate hunters for all or most of their careers.

Jordan was an ivory poacher.

He had many names. In East Africa he was *Bwana Mkuba*—the "big Bwana." He was also *Koufiwa Simba Sitani* — "slayer of the Devil Lion." To the Maasai, he was *Eldama Elmoran*— "the Elephant Warrior." The Lumbwa, who have since become the Kipsogi, called him *Mongaso* — "the man who is always moving," and that was the name that stuck.

Like Selous and John Boyes and so many others before him, Jordan began his career on the Dark Continent in South Africa, enlisting in the Cape Mounted Police. And, like Selous and Boyes and the rest, an urge to see what lay beyond the next hill, a driving curiosity coupled with a sense of adventure, got him moving north until he wound up in Kenya, where almost all the great hunters and adventurers seemed to wind up sooner or later. For years he poached elephants on both sides of the Kenya-Tanganyika border (which was then the border between British East Africa and German East Africa). He seemed to take a special delight in poaching ivory on German territory.

Things didn't always, or even often, go smoothly for Jordan. Over the years he took a bullet, a Nandi spear, and a green mamba bite in the same leg. He often had to flee for his life, not from animals but officials. His health never stayed good for very long. When he finally married, he and his bride decided to take the first cross-continent safari in African history, starting at the Indian Ocean and ending 4,000 miles away at the Atlantic. During that honeymoon, the white men who were accompanying them all quit before the journey was half done, most of the porters deserted, Jordan himself came down with an endless series of tropical diseases, and his wife became so ill that she had to leave Africa, never to return.

I discovered this book when I was a young man, in my teens, and the beauty of the prose stayed with me for forty years. The reason, it turns out, is simple: Jordan didn't write it. He experienced it, and most of it has been authenticated through photos and documents, but it was an "as-told-to" book, written by the brilliant John Prebble, author of such stellar fiction as *Age Without Pity* and *White Feather*. As you'll see, the opening chapter is practically a prose poem.

(There is only one reason that *Elephants and Ivory* did not appear earlier in this series: it took me five years to track down the rights.)

Foreword

By the way, Jordan's experiences do not end with this book (which was published first in England as *Mongaso*, then here as *Elephants and Ivory*). He "wrote" another "as-told-to" book called *The Elephant Stone* — and perhaps someday we'll publish it in this series...but it is inferior to this one, mainly because he didn't tell it to Prebble but to someone else.

This book will tell you, through Jordan's memory and Prebble's evocative prose, of the many experiences he underwent. You'll see gorillas cry over the loss of a family member. You'll learn bushcraft from the Wanderobo — who, according to my own African guide, the redoubtable Perry Mason, "could track a billard ball down a concrete highway". You'll watch Jordan kill crocodiles from sheer hatred until he was sated and could kill no more. You'll see him befriend the Maasai, and become the overlord of two thousand Lumbwa spearmen.

Since he was a devout believer in the myths of Africa, you'll search with him for the Elephant Stone. You'll join him as he goes into the bush, seeking yet another legend, the *jablunketmachoies*, a tribe whose warriors were said to be half- man and half-leopard. You'll walk side by side with him as he goes hunting for the *dingonek*, a creature as broad as a hippo, spotted like a leopard, with a crocodile's head.

And always, always, you'll accompany him as he goes after the "Big Ones," the huge bull elephants carrying one hundred pounds in each tusk.

But of them all, I think the one story that will remain with you, as it did with me, is Jordan's parable of the little brown honey bird, and its promise of all things beautiful.

I found Jordan so fascinating that I appropriated him for my science fiction novel *Paradise*, where he appears as August Hardwycke. If you don't find him equally fascinating, if his story doesn't make you nostalgic for an Africa that once was and will never be again, I'll be very much surprised and more than a little disappointed.

— Mike Resnick,
Series Editor

✳ C O N T E N T S ✳

Elephants and Ivory

*

ONE

The Little Brown Honey Bird

My Africa is gone, said Jordan. If I knew it like a book it is now an old book, and its pages are yellow. I have seen a thousand elephants herded in the Semiliki Valley in the noon sun. Their trunks hanging idle, only their ears moving against the flies. I have killed forty crocodile in one day on Victoria Nyanza. I killed crocodile because I hated them, not just for the three rupees a head that the Germans were paying. Nothing else I killed like that.

I expected to die in Africa. When I was young, this expectation did not worry me; perhaps there was a consolation in it, for I did not think of myself as an exile and I had no longing to return to England. I always believed that I would die in Africa, maybe that day or the next, and several times I should have died. I had malaria many times. I had blackwater fever. I was bitten by a green mamba and I was speared by the Kisi. It all happened fifty years ago and I am still alive.

When I first went to Nairobi I was twenty-one and I saw lions in the streets at night. They were old gray-manes, too old to pull down a zebra any more, and they had turned to eating men. There was little in Nairobi

in those days but the old Stanley Hotel and Tommy
Woods' store, before the settlers took up land in the
Kikuyu country. There were not more than a hundred
Europeans in the town, but you could see Sikhs, Parsees,
Somalis and Goanese, Hindu women in rainbow saris,
Arabs carrying flintlocks that were inlaid with silver,
Kikuyu dandies with the lobes of their ears split and
distended to hold porcelain ointment jars, Wakamba in
red blankets with their teeth filed to remind you that
they had been and perhaps still were cannibals. You
could see old John Boyes, who was a great man among
the Kikuyu, riding a small Abyssinian mule. And there
were over a million acres of good land waiting for the
plough.

I am the last of my Africa, I think, the last of the
hunters who made my Africa, that is. The others are still
there, in the graveyard at Nairobi, and perhaps you can
no longer read what brought them there: Killed by
a lion. . . . Killed by a buffalo. . . . Killed by the
Nandi. . . .

They were all nationalities, and hard, the men you
would find on any frontier, and many of them had seen
all the frontiers that were left fifty years ago. They were
Englishmen, Greeks, Australasians, Scots, Irish, Ameri-
cans and Canadians, and they created little legends that
nobody ever recorded. When Pearson was mauled by a
lion he wrestled with it, punching it until his friend
Tarletan could shoot it. There was Banks, one of the
few men I knew who were tossed by a buffalo and lived.
There was Boyes, who went alone among the Kikuyu.
There was Will Judd, who was a great hunter, and there

was Selous, who was the greatest hunter there has ever been.

There was at one time a native republic between Uganda and the Belgian Congo where the askaris never patrolled. It was made up of outcasts from the tribes, army deserters, petty criminals. It was a good country to hunt in, though the natives did not welcome you. But a Scots hunter called Gordon went up there, and they caught him. They stripped him and spread-eagled him between two posts, and they flayed his back with rhino whips. Then they were frightened by what they had done and they let him go. They should not have let him go, for he came back to Nairobi and hired some Somalis and armed them with old Sniders, and he went back to that republic and killed everyone he could find and burned their villages. The Belgians and the British put a price on his head. The askaris found his camp, and he was shot as he ran for the bush.

You might think your nationality would not matter on a frontier, but you could have your ribs kicked in just for being a Greek, or an Australian or an Englishman. There was always somebody who wanted to fight. They made their own laws. There was a man, an Englishman I think, who shot and killed a Somali walking across his land. It was murder, of course, but the jury brought in a verdict of not guilty.

If I remember those things, I remember others. In the Lumbwa highlands there were clear, musical waters like English trout streams. I have come upon them suddenly, and seen the pale green moss, the orchids, the filigree ferns, and I have sat down and watched the butterflies and sworn that there was where I would stay. But I have always moved on. I have waited a week just to see the mist lift from the lovely granite Mountains of the Moon, and yet I have moved on.

On the plains below Kilimanjaro, where that mountain once cut a notch into British territory, I have ridden down and roped giraffe like a Western cowboy. The snow leopard is more common up there by the crest of Kilimanjaro than Mr. Hemingway would have you believe, and on the slopes of Kilimanjaro was found the biggest elephant tusk in the world, weighing nearly 220 pounds, I believe, and I always wanted to find one greater.

There was so much fish in Lake Barango that the crocodile had no taste for human flesh, and I have sat on the banks and watched the *endito,* the beautiful young women of the Enjemps Masai, their skins like wet chocolate as they swam in the lake among the crocodile.

On the plains the dry, yellow canes of the elephant grass grow to fifteen feet, and the only way you can pass through them is to follow the tracks of the tuskers or the tunnels the rhino make. Yet there are meadows on the Loita plains where the grass is short and like wild timothy, slashed by the dark green of reeds. The mimosa trees have white thorns like sabers, and the fishhooks of the thornbushes have to be cut out of your flesh with a skinning knife. The beauty of Africa is a kernel within a cruel shell. The eczema never healed on my leg, the leg that took a Boer bullet, a mamba bite and a Kisi spear. Sometimes the pain of it was so bad that I would hold the leg in the fire, or scrape it with my knife.

There are things I cannot explain about Africa, and do not want explained to me. One day at dusk I wounded a lion, and the sun went down before I could find it and kill it. That night the lions came up to the camp and sat around it, roaring. There was an old man of the Wanderobo among my trackers, and he came to me and said, "I will get rid of them, Bwana." I said, all right, go ahead.

He took some dust from a pouch at his waist and sprinkled it on the palm of his left hand. Then he stood in the center of our camp and solemnly puffed the dust toward the darkness, and one by one the lions were silent.

Old Koydelot, a witch doctor of the Wanderobo, would squat before me in the morning, rattling his stones in a calabash, and spilling them in the dust before his knees. From the way they fell he would read the luck we would have in our shooting that day, and he was always right.

There is the little brown honey bird. Anybody who has been in Africa—anyone, that is, who steps outside Nairobi or Mombasa—will tell you about the little brown honey bird. He is like a sparrow and as friendly. He'll come to your camp and call to you, or he'll call to you when you are on trek, and you leave it to your boys for they know what to do. As they step toward him, he will fly up and lead them to a hive, and wait while they gather grass and smoke out the bees. But some of the honey must be left for him, for if you take it all then the next time he calls to you he will lead you into an ambush, to a waiting leopard perhaps. This I believe,

for I know it to be true. And the invitation of the honey
bird was Africa's welcome to me, and the honey he
invited me to share with him was the richness I found
there.

There were one hundred thousand square miles of
the Ituri forest in my day, cedar, acacia, juniper, ma-
hogany trees like the pillars in a cathedral nave, and it
was beautiful and ugly, and peaceful and menacing. In
parts of it the pigmies lived, and there you had to be
content with making no more than four miles a day
through the trees, for the pigmies planted their traps
cunningly and instead of the elephant it could be you
who fell into their cone pits, or were transfixed by a
weighted spear.

There were cannibals in the Ituri. The first story a
newcomer to Nairobi was told was of the missionary
whom the Manjama from the Djiji district kept pegged
out in a stream for two days after they had speared
him, until his flesh was ready to eat. But I never knew
whether this story was true, and there are always men
who enjoy the irreligious irony of missionaries being
eaten before they have time to open their Bibles. I did
not like cannibals any more than I liked the crocodile.
They did not eat the old people of their own tribe, but
went into the catering business, selling them to other
tribes. An old man, a dead man, means nothing to the
natives anyway, and perhaps they are right for the body
is meaningless once the spirit is gone. Most tribes throw
their dead into the bush for the hyena, and this is not a
good practice for it also gives an old gray lion a taste for
man.

I remember the plains, the yellow grass and the red earth, and the blue sky, and the trees that seemed more black than green, punched down by the wind. It was fine to see a young Masai *elmoran* going out alone into this loneliness with his spear and his bow and his sword and his buffalo shield, to make himself a man by killing a lion. I have seen such an *elmoran,* his long hair fastidiously dressed with red clay and castor oil, shouting and jeering at a black mane lion, and I have seen the lion lope away like a dog. Nine times out of ten you can face a lion down, even drive it away from its kill, and that I have seen the Lumbwa do as well as the Masai. But it is worth thinking of the tenth time.

I was never lonely. I would be away in the forest for two years, and when I returned to Kericho or Nairobi, I found it hard to put my tongue to English. The Lumbwa called me *Mongaso,* which means "The Man Who Is Always Moving." That is how a man should be when he is young, for when he is old his bones and his heart will see to it that he cannot move, perhaps not even out of his chair as is the way with me now, sometimes.

The Lumbwa who called me Mongaso were my friends. Mataia and Arab Changalla, chiefs of the Manga and the Setick Lumbwa, were my brothers and they made me overlord of one thousand of their young *elmorani.*

I had the reputation of being the worst ivory poacher in East Africa. In one season along the upper Maggori I traded ivory for much cattle to Greek traders in German territory, and this was against the law which allowed you no more than two elephants on one license, and the Germans would have shot me had they caught me. I could not see who owned the elephant. One day he would be in German East, a week later he would be grazing in Kisi province, and no one had put a label on him to say that this was a German elephant or a British elephant.

There is much killing in my story, but I slaughtered nothing except crocodile. I would follow an elephant herd for months to get the tusks I wanted, and I never killed a cow elephant unless she made me. The killing of cows was for men with no pride, the men who put down donkey bait and shot lion from a tree. There were men who would shoot a cow elephant even after the game laws said that they might kill no more than two elephants, and surely when a man's choice is thus limited he should be satisfied with the best only.

I killed many elephants and many other animals, and because I was a professional hunter I brought no trophies out of Africa, and there is no tangible thing I can show to prove that I am speaking the truth when I say I have done this or that, and where I am wrong, as I surely must be wrong here and there, it is because my memory, like my body, has grown old.

✳ T W O ✳

The Big Ones

There is a strange thing about the elephants, said Jordan. In a storm I have seen them covering their tusks with their ears, bringing the great flaps forward like a cape. The lightning can strike their ivory. I believe this because once I saw a lone bull taking shelter in a storm, his ears forward over his face, yet this did not save him. When the storm had gone and the sun came out I went to where he had seen standing, and there I found a tusk newly broken off, and it weighed sixty-four pounds.

There is another strange thing about the elephant. Only once did I see one lying down, like a cow in a field. I thought he was dead until he got the scent of me and rose up. Natives told me that they had never seen the Big Ones lying down, and this is strange when you think how long the elephant can live, and lives it all on his feet.

They are wonderful animals and I have a great love and admiration for them, which may seem odd to you, thinking that I shot them for their ivory. But you have to see them to understand what I mean, when a herd of them is hull down on a yellow ridge and then something sets them moving and the sun comes suddenly on their tusks, and a bull trumpets, and that is a sound like nothing else you have ever heard, for it is a sound you *feel* as much as hear. You feel it in your stomach, you feel it as it moves up and catches your throat. Once the world must have been full of more terrible sounds, when the elephant was outnumbered and outmastered by animals that are now only Latin names and plaster casts in a museum. But the elephant has survived them all and trumpets his pride.

The herd comes on slowly, gently, ears like great sails, like a great fleet of great frigates, coming down, swaying and swinging until they halt again, and now there is no sound but the wrench of grass as they tear it up, and, if you like impudent paradoxes, the rumble of their stomachs. All elephants have indigestion, and this is the most uncharitable practical joke in zoology.

But think of their ivory. Thirty inches of it in the skull before it begins to curve outward for another six feet, and threaded with a nerve that you pull out like a cord. The top part of the skull is empty, a great and mysterious vacuum, and every time I saw a native axe beating its way into this silent hollow I felt uneasy and sometimes ashamed.

Elephants are left-handed. I mean that they use the left tusk for digging and rooting, so that you never get a perfectly matched pair of tusks, the left is always shorter than the right. On a big bull the foot can be five feet in circumference, cushioned with layers of fat between layers of bone, yet in movement the elephant is dainty and silent, lifting his feet and putting them down as softly as a young lady in a minuet. I have followed a big herd into long grass or a forest and heard nothing, not a sound of them, until I broke through to the other side and saw them two miles away, grazing. Placid and unquarrelsome, myopic and incurious, they do not seek to determine their mastery, yet nothing dares attack them. I have never seen a clawing lion hanging from an elephant's shoulder; the lion knows better than that. Nothing will attack an elephant but man, and only man can make him savage and relentless.

Craig Helkett was a young officer in the King's African Rifles, and one year, many years ago, he decided to kill an elephant before he went home on furlough. He caught a bull with a mortal chest shot, but left the firing of it too late so that the bull came on him. It thrust one of its tusks through Helkett's stomach, and then through his thigh, and it picked him up and threw him into the bush, and then stood there and died.

It took two weeks, day and night, for his boys to carry Helkett into Entebbe, and yet he lived.

There are things I believe about the elephant, and there are things I do not believe. I have never seen the Elephant Graveyard and I do not believe that it exists. The elephant dies where he dies, and he does not walk to find his cemetery, even to please the romantics, and if you ask why then are not his bones found the answer is that they are. They are found by the vulture, the hyena, the lion and the wild dog, and these take the meat. They are found by the native, the grassfire and the bush storm, and these take the ivory and destroy the bones.

But this I know about a dying elephant: If you

have wounded one and he feels the dying inside him he will thrust his head deep into a thorn bush, as if he knew that you had killed him for his ivory and that the thorns, as you cut out the tusks, will repay him a little with your suffering.

He is wise. He will not step over a trench, be it as shallow as your hand, but, suspecting traps, will walk a mile along its length until it is gone. And although the flies breed and live on his little eyes, his scent and hearing are miraculous.

These things I believe about the elephant. I do not believe in the rogue elephant, the outlaw, although perhaps it is just that I have never seen one. But I have seen a herd with its scouts out, young bulls on the perimeter watching, and this only among elephants who have met man. I have seen elephants pick up a wounded bull, pick him up, I say, between their barrel bodies and carry him away, while the young bulls stand between you and the herd with their trunks up in a swan's neck.

This, too, I can tell you about the elephant. A friend of mine was killed by a cow elephant and when she had killed him, she broke off young branches and covered his dead body with them.

I shot elephant with a .500 Express. It was the best gun I knew, although I also used a single-barreled .600 that can knock down a five-ton elephant, not that it is always a matter of one shot and posing for your picture with your foot on its neck. I once put twenty-nine bullets into a bull before he went down, and I am not proud of that.

But a .600 is good for thick country where you can be within five or six yards of your animal before you get a chance to fire and you've got to knock it down or lose it. Occasionally I used a Canadian .280 with a pointed round, and for open country a .256 Mannlicher, although not against elephant. Yet Selous once said he preferred the higher velocity and flat trajectory of the Mannlicher against elephant, but Selous was Selous. A bullet in an African animal means little to it at the time of the hit, except something that makes it run the harder, away from you or toward you. You must get a brain or a heart or a spine shot, and when I was hunting with a Texan rancher called Bronson I saw him put nine .35 Mauser bullets into a hartebeest before it stopped running and died. On Victoria Nyanza the first officer of the steamer *Clement Hill* fired twenty-two .303's into a hippo before killing it, which was ignorant and senseless, for you shoot a hippo through the nostril as it yawns at you, and the bullet passes into its brainpan. With each successive shot I was forced to fire at a badly hit animal my shame increased.

Those were the weapons I carried, and sometimes I had a Webley .45 as a side arm, but this was merely an affectation and I got along too well with the natives to have to frighten them with a revolver. I had a skinning knife at the back of my belt and I carried a *reongu* —a straightened rhino horn club which cannot be destroyed, except by fire.

There was little more a hunter needed—a double-fly tent, camp bed and netting. In twenty-five years I never slept in a native hut. And it was a good life. My

chop boxes carried tea and coffee and sugar and salt.
I shot my meat, eland, impala, antelope. I've sat in the
bush and had dinner of guinea fowl with a tin cup of
wine, and thought myself more fortunate than anyone
at Delmonico's.

I was an ivory poacher and that was too long ago
for anyone to do anything about it now, anyone with
the exaggerated respect for the law you find in frightened people. Elephant poaching began long ago, too,
long before I was a boy and went off to find adventure
with the Cape Mounted in the Boer War. The Arabs
turned to the business when slave-running became too
costly and too dangerous. Then they became the middle
men and white men did the shooting. Game licenses
came with the sportsmen, and with the game laws
came the game rangers, and after the rangers came the
railways and the roads and the towns and the film
makers, but by then I had gone from Africa.

I always had a license for elephant. I have one
still, made out to me in the Belgian Congo by the
Bureau of Bandundu: *Permis de Chasse pour l'éléphant.
Taxe 1000 Francs. Durée de validité: un an. Délivré
à Monsieur J. A. Jordan. Valable pour tout le téritoire.*
That is what it says.

The independent elephant hunter was in instinctive rebellion against this sort of thing. For years he
had been content to take his life in his own hands, shoot
his elephant without permission, live in fever swamps,
go alone among the Nandi and the Kisi, trade his ivory,
get drunk in Kericho and Nairobi, fight when he wanted
to, die the way he chose. He was made a poacher by

the game laws. He shot for profit. He had no home. He had no library wall to stud with the horns of kudu and rhino. He was in Africa for life, not for the season.

There was Jones who killed a leopard with his hands after he had shot her. She came back along her own blood trail and she leaped on him. He got his knee in her ribs and crushed her and killed her for he was a big man, but not before she had bitten through his thigh and left him with a limp to remember her by.

When Banks was tossed by that buffalo, he clung to a mimosa tree and stayed there until the bull went away. He was badly gored and deaf forever. It did not stop his poaching. His gunbearer became his ears, keeping beside Banks and signaling with his hands.

There was a South African hunter called Deacon. When poaching along the Belgian border, he was caught and taken to Beni. The Belgians took away his equipment, his rifles and six tusks, and they let him go because they had no jail in which to hold a white man. They told him to trek back to British territory thirty miles away and they did not want to see him in Beni again. But he waited out in the forest until night, and then he came back, and he gagged and bound four sentries, released his boys from jail, broke into the store and took his rifles and tusks, and by a forced march was over the border by sunrise.

There was a Canadian who was wealthy enough to live safely at home, but he added to his private income of fifteen thousand dollars a year by ivory-poaching. A native sergeant and four askaris caught him in Belgian territory one day, and when he refused

to go with them the sergeant raised his rifle. The Canadian pulled out his revolver and killed the soldier. Then
he held up the askaris and made them march before
him to the Nile, where he crossed over. The Belgians demanded his extradition, but found themselves
blocked by the law which did not allow a native
policeman to arrest a white man.

With elephant grazing in thousands across the
Semiliki, I could make three or four thousand pounds
a year, and this is fifty years ago. All up the Inzia the
elephants were always plentiful, but their tusks were
narrow and worn to sharp points because the soil was
gravelly where they rooted. But there was good killing
and this will show you how good for one summer:

July: Nine bulls averaging 20 kilo tusks, value
6,500 francs. August: Seven bulls averaging 25 kilo
tusks. September: fourteen bulls averaging 30 kilo tusks.
October: eighteen bulls, averaging 40 kilo tusks. I was
lucky with the Big Ones.

Once I took a concession of fifty-five thousand
acres in the Thysville area, and it was about that time
that I was ready in my elephant fever to believe a
Frenchman when he told me that there were water-
elephant. He said that he had seen them swimming
in Lake Leopold like hippo. Then I knew it was a
dream out of ignorance, for all elephant love water. I
have seen them crossing a river full of crocodile in the
Belgian Congo, going down to the water like a regiment, bulls, cows and calves, and into the strong current and out the other side. They are good road makers,
good ford finders.

It was in that country that I came across my King Elephant. He must have been thirteen feet at the shoulders, and his tusks would have been a record had I been able to kill him. This you must believe, for I have seen thousands of elephant and shot many bulls.

Yet when the King came out of the grass I could not shoot. The sun was behind him and his shadow fell across me. When he saw me his ears came out like the opening of doors, his trunk swung up and he trumpeted. I aimed for his ear and fired, but it was a bad shot. If it hit him at all, it glanced across his skull, but it turned him and I saw a great white scar like a saber-cut on his shoulder. He went off and I followed him. I found the marks of his tusks where he had pulled himself up the slopes, and I followed him until midday but never close enough to fire again. He crossed the waters of the Kuilo like a barge, and there was no way I could follow him.

My boys said he was a ghost elephant, and that they had wounded him often with their muzzle-loaders, and I wanted that King Elephant as I had wanted nothing else. I saw him often and never killed him. One morning I tracked him and saw him, but he knew I was there, and he trumpeted and went down the other side of the ridge. I swore and ran after him and fell over a root. The jolt fired my Express and when I picked it up, I found that one barrel was split two inches at the muzzle where it had been choked with dust.

The King had that sort of luck. I thought I should go home. Then I thought: There's one more barrel to

the gun. So I went on. I saw him again, five hundred
yards off, switching his ears at the flies on his eyes. I
tried to head him off but he beat me by fifty yards. I
was in a temper, which is no state to be in if you wish
to shoot an elephant. I gave him a slanting shot, hoping
this would slow him before he took to the river, and
I rammed another round into the breech. But he had
gone over the water into the tall grass and between us
was the river with the crocodile rippling it.

And when I looked at my gun I saw that the
second barrel had worked loose. Had I fired another
shot, it would have blown up in my face. I never did
shoot the King. Perhaps no one did. He was an im-
mortal.

I would spend days watching elephants, not wanting to shoot them, just wanting to watch them. I have
seen them put out a grass fire. I have seen them
methodically trample out each flame until the fire was
gone and there was only black earth. I have seen a
herd coming over a cliff face in play, scores of them,
sliding down on their rumps like schoolboys, hundreds
of them making a black waterfall in the red dust, trumpeting and trilling.

I have seen a herd scatter at danger and yet re-
group uncannily twenty miles on in the grass, and this
with the range of their fly-encrusted eyes no more than
thirty yards. I have seen them at the salt licks where
they dig up the earth and eat it, and where the sportsmen wait for them comfortably in blinds. But not
always comfortably for sometimes the bulls will form
into line like cavalry and charge the blinds.

For years I believed I knew one certain thing about the elephant. I believed that it would not charge into a small island of trees. Even the young ones seemed to know that such a place might contain a trap pit, or that in the branches above was a poised spear, held fast in a log. So when a cow elephant scented me one day, and came up surlily to mark me out, I ran to such an island of trees for safety. But she came in after me with trunk searching and I had to kill her.

I have a great respect for the elephant, that grass eater.

I believe in the Elephant Stone, although I have never seen it. In New York I once talked with dealers of precious gems, and while some had heard of the Elephant Stone none had ever seen it. But the natives believed in it, and I heard them speak of a Swahili trader who bought one from a Loita Masai for much money and cattle. But the Swahili trader and the Loita Masai were dead, and you could not find them, but always there was somebody in a Masai *munyata* who knew of the Stone. They respected it and said it brought death, for the Swahili had been killed by a leopard and the Masai by a buffalo, which are both terrible deaths.

The Elephant Stone will be found, when it is found, up there in an elephant's skull, and if you see a bull without tusks maybe that bull is carrying the Stone in the temple of his great head, for the tusks have not grown outward, if you understand me, but inward, inward to form this hard stone of great beauty, just as an oyster grows a pearl.

I was once told that the Wanderobo had found

such a stone behind the eye socket of a great bull, but I never found it. I do not know what it looks like, except that it is larger than the Koh-i-noor and glitters more wondrously.

I once shot a tuskless bull when I was with the Wanderobo, a great bull that lay all night in the forest, and I sweated as I waited for the morning when the skull could be cleft open. In the morning the Wanderobo cut into the skull with their axes and there, at the right side of the skull, where the tusk should start, was a large ball of ivory about the size and shape of a cocoanut. I hacked at it with a hatchet, believing it to be the shell of the Stone, and in the end I had nothing but splinters and shavings of ivory, for there was no Stone.

But it is my fancy to believe that it exists.

In the Kisumu Province, by the shores of Lake Victoria, when I was young, I was camped by the house of a Dutchman with whom I drank in the evening and talked about the Cape. He had a husky brother who came up from Londiani Station and this brother wanted to shoot an elephant for he had shot nothing larger than eland and when a man has shot an elephant his life is full. So I said that I would take him to shoot his elephant if he would pay the expenses. All I wanted was half the ivory.

But I had picked the wrong Dutchman. On our first night out, by a Masai *munyata,* he took a young girl and the warriors wanted to spear him there. I talked with the old men where they sat in their blankets in the dust, and I made them presents and I told them that the Dutchman had been drunk and this excuse they accepted and talked their *elmorani* out of killing. But to the Dutchman I said other things, and he took my anger badly, but I did not then realize how badly.

On the third day we struck fresh elephant spoor, their tracks and the tall cones of their droppings, and we followed this until dusk, and again the next morning, with the trail going across the bare Kidon Valley. I looked into the ripple of the heat haze and could not see them. I knew they were making for the Seli Lake and I knew we should find them there.

There was only one tree in the valley, one tree that you could call a tree, black and squat, and we camped beneath it for the night. My Dutchman had spoken little to me since we left the Masai *munyata* and as the lions began to cough beyond the rim of our fire, I watched his face. He was listening for the lions and he was listening for them hard, hearing them before they roared and when they did roar his lips twitched. I went to sleep and left him to his imagination while the lions chased the zebra in the dark.

I was awakened by the sound of rhino, the angry squeal of it and the roll of its hoofs and I came out of my tent quickly with my gun, afraid, for the rhino, who needs glasses in the daylight, has cat's eyes at night and loves to charge a camp.

I threw brushwood on the fire and as it flared up I saw the rhino draped in the Dutchman's tent as if it were a coat, snorting, plunging, stabbing with its three-foot horn. I aimed at it and paused, struck by the intriguing notion that as well as wearing the tent the rhino might well be wearing the Dutchman too.

Then he shouted at me from the tree above, "Shoot, damn you, shoot!"

The rhino now had his head free from the canvas and was standing there in the firelight, blowing through his nose and staring at me from behind his horn. So I fired both barrels of the Express and saw the dust come out of his hide. He went down on his knees, pushing up the earth with his jaw, and died.

The Dutchman stayed in the tree and would not come down. I called for my boys and they came out of the darkness, looking at the rhino, looking at the tree and grinning. They told me. They said that after I had gone to sleep the roaring of the lions had worried the Dutchman even more and he had gone from boy to boy telling them to go out and drive the lions away, until they left him in disgust and built another fire a hundred yards off. Left alone he had climbed the tree and watched the rhino come out of the brush.

It was first light and I told my cook boy to make some coffee, and the smell of this brought the Dutchman down out of his tree, in a temper about the loss of his tent which he seemed to think was my fault.

I was sorry he was so afraid.

The morning brought us the sight of elephant, down the rise half a mile away, about fifty of them, like a group of black hillocks in the grass. I said I would go forward and the Dutchman should follow me at an interval.

The elephants were stretched along the bottom of

a little rise and my gunbearer and I worked round until we were facing them, and then we sat down in the grass to wait for the Dutchman. I saw him coming, about five hundred yards away, and I stood up and waved my hat to him, and perhaps he saw me and perhaps he didn't. But when he saw the elephant beyond us he opened fire.

His first and second bullets went over our heads and we lay down in the grass. The elephant shook their ears at the sound of the Dutchman's gun and went off, and with them went my chance of getting their ivory which, I told myself, was the only reason why I was tolerating this idiot. I stood up and waved again, and now he fired several shots. I called the boy and told him to creep up to the Dutchman, and if the bwana looked sane enough to understand, to acquaint him with the situation.

The Dutchman came up full of apologies. He said that he thought we were lions. He was very much afraid of lions, this Dutchman.

I gave him my .500 to carry and asked him to tread boldly in my footsteps, and we went after the herd again. We got to within fifty yards of it, and it was led by a fine old tusker who was pushing the glory of his ivory before him. I fired with the Mannlicher and if I hit him, it did him no harm, but the herd rippled and a young bull broke off from it and came at us, ears wide like a mainsail, trunk up, pink triangle of a mouth red.

I turned to take the .500 from the Dutchman, but he had gone and so had the boys. I had time for one more shot with the Mannlicher and then threw myself on the ground. The thud of his charge jarred my chin, and I waited for him to trample me, and it was as if I waited a year before I would take my face out of the dirt and lift it to see the motionless grass and the sky, lift it higher until I saw my bull about thirty yards away, standing still, square on his feet, tusks up, trunk curled, but wondering where I had got to. He was very close and I shot at his heart. He gave a forward plunge and swayed, but he did not go down. Then, sadly almost, he moved off into the grass.

My boys came up, and the Dutchman was behind them, staring at me as if he were surprised to find me still alive. I shared his surprise.

I didn't like the look of the grass, the black profile of the elephant's spine above it. We could hear him breathing as he fought the bullet inside him.

I climbed the lower branches of a mimosa to see him the better, and I disturbed some honeybees and they spun around me, stinging me on the neck and face and arms. I swore at them and began to come down, and as I moved the young bull swerved out of the grass blowing delicate bubbles of blood. He saw me and charged. I fired. The recoil threw me from the branch and we came down to earth together, but he was dead.

The boys took an hour to draw out the stings, and it was kind of them to do that before they took the honey from the hive as their sweet share of the day's comedy. The Dutchman watched the stings being plucked out with that stare of impersonal curiosity you see on people's faces at a road accident. When the last sting was out, he remarked that he had not yet shot his elephant. I told him to supervise the cutting-out of the tusks. I felt that this was about as close to shooting an elephant as he would ever get.

He hunted zebra the next day and made a great killing. The day following he spent drying their skins. On the third day I decided that we could do worse than go after lion. If he shot one, he might be less embarrassed by their music at night.

We went over a swamp toward the hills. It was then, I believe, that the Dutchman discovered murder in his heart and was not shocked by the discovery.

He saw the lioness first and called to me. She was a tawny beauty, in silent lope, carrying a pig in her mouth, with her ears back. My Dutchman's shout alarmed her. She dropped the pig and went back on her haunches. And the pig, still alive with its back unbroken, twinkled off, running straight at us, through my legs and throwing me. As I fell I heard my Dutchman fire, and I rolled over to see the lioness going into the grass.

I found no blood spoor but I felt charitable. He could have hit her. I was beating the grass to make sure when I heard him fire again, and I went over. He was sitting on his heel staring across the stream. He said he had shot the lioness, but when I went over I found a leopard, a fine male, with a bullet through its chest. He deserved congratulations for that shot, even though he had mistaken a leopard for a lioness, and so I congratulated him and I told him I would go down and get the boys to bring the leopard in.

I had reached the thick reeds when his shot took

my helmet from my head. It is never wise to become
hysterical when this sort of thing happens, so I lay down
to think about it. And having thought, I became angry.
I crawled on my knees and skirted the reeds until I had
the Dutchman in view at close range. He was sitting
there with his gun on his thighs staring at the spot
where he had last seen me, and perhaps he was wondering whether he had killed me. I fired two shots at him,
close enough for him to feel them passing. He sat quite
still. I put two more shots over his head and was pleased
to hear him scream. He went on screaming until I
walked out, carrying my helmet, with my forefinger
through the hole he had put in it.

He sulked, and I had had enough of him and
this elephant hunt, which had turned out to be no
elephant hunt at all.

I put some cartridges in my pocket and went to
shoot the marabout storks that would be feeding on
the maggots in the dead bull, and I was bad enough
or bad-tempered enough to leave it too late to find my
way back to the camp.

I decided to light a fire and stay there the night.
I was the Great White Hunter, the Bwana Mkuba, but
I had no matches in my pocket and no skill with fire
sticks. I had to go back. Or stay in the darkness, a free
gift to any lion. So I walked, and as I walked, I knew
there was very little chance of finding the camp. I
walked on the ridges looking for the glow of the fire, and
perhaps I would have seen it eventually, or perhaps I
would not, but for the rhino.

One moment there was silence, just the rustle of

my boots in the grass. The next moment the rhino was behind me, breathing like a shunting engine. I did not wait for him to scent me, I ran. Of all the points of the compass I could have chosen to run, the one I chose instinctively in my fear led me to the camp, with my boys leaping up as I came upon it, and shouting.

I went to bed without speaking to the Dutchman. For all I knew he might have been in another tree.

We went back to Londiani the next morning. I left the Dutchman without sorrow. He took up land in the Nandi country, and I heard the Nandi killed him. This could be so, for the *endito* of the Nandi are as beautiful as any Masai maiden.

✳ T H R E E ✳

Labusoni's Elephant Hunt

I liked to hunt elephant with the Wanderobo, said Jordan.

They were a fierce little people without fear and without shame. They would attack any animal, any man. I mean the true Wanderobo, the *shenzi*, the wild men of the forest. All fighting tribes have their wanderobo, their outcasts, men who take to the forest to escape punishment for crimes, and there they live until they are killed.

The true Wanderobo I remember as great hunters, and although they may have begun as did the outcasts of the tribes, when I knew the true Wanderobo, they were a people in their own right. They made no villages but wandered along the elephant paths in parties of ten or fifteen, living in holes or caves, or trees, or shelters they made by bending saplings together and covering them with leaves. Yet they were linked loosely together into tribal communities under chiefs, the greatest of whom was Labusoni. They wore capes of gazelle and monkey skins, tied with antelope sinews, and they were naked but for these capes. They were so much like animals that when they drank they would go down on their hands and knees and lap up the water.

30

They did not make a cup of their hands, or throw water into their open mouths, the way you will see a Masai cleanly drinking. They were like animals, and when captured they would foam at the mouth and tear at the bonds with their teeth like a leopard, and curse in a gabbling mixture of Masai and Lumbwa and the chatter of apes.

But they were hunters, and nowhere in Africa was their equal as trackers. They carried six-foot bows that dwarfed them. In their monkey-skin quivers they had arrows smeared with poison. They carried two-edged swords and could drive them through the skin of a charging rhino.

I went among them from the noble Lumbwa who were warriors and arrogant aristocrats like the Nandi and the Masai. I had been trading cattle among the Lumbwa for sheep, and trading the sheep for rhino horn, and doing good business for a man who preferred to shoot elephant, and because I preferred to shoot elephant, I went up among the Wanderobo and I liked them, which you may not find easy to understand. But I lived alone and hunted alone with the Wanderobo, and when they were hungry I was hungry, and I wept with them at the visitation of fire and famine and disease. In such experiences do you discover friends.

Perhaps they are gone now as I knew them. I know they are gone, for there are books that speak of the Wanderobo contemptuously as unreliable and cowardly trackers. I saw my first tractor in Africa in 1912, and I saw the end of the Wanderobo with it. Now they

ride on the running boards of the lorries that take men
to shoot elephants, and this is something that would
have sickened Labusoni's stomach. I never knew such
bravery as I saw in the Wanderobo. I have killed many
elephants, but I killed them with a .500 Express, and
I do not think I would have had the guts to kill them
as the *shenzi* did.

This is how I came to the Wanderobo:

I had been pursuing a private and bitter war
against the crocodile on the Maggori river, and when I
killed enough to satisfy my hatred, I went back to Port
Florence. And perhaps shooting crocodile from the
safety of a river bank had made me ashamed of myself
and I told myself that I was going soft. So I rode the
train to Lumbwa Station and then trekked for the Loita
plains where the Masai lived.

I wanted some Lumbwa *elmorani* to come with
me, but although they are much like the Masai and
respect each other, they are jealous of each other too
and are not above settling such jealousy with their
swords. So the Lumbwa I asked were full of excuses,
and would not come. I got their chief to bully twenty
of his warriors into accepting, and when they had finished shrugging their shoulders and thudding the hafts
of their spears in the dust, they said they would come,
but I must be careful of the Wanderobo who lived in
the forest. And I did not tell them that it was the
Wanderobo I wanted to meet.

We met them after we had crossed the river and
were sitting on its banks in the sunlight and the shadow.
We heard a sharp whistle in the forest behind us, and

an *elmoran* shuffled over to me and whispered, "*Shenzi,*
Bwana." I told the Lumbwa to go out and bring me a
Wanderobo, and they looked at me, but they went.

They were out two hours and when they came in
they brought a man and boy. The Wanderobo stood
there with the tall Lumbwa about them, and the man
said he understood both the Lumbwa and Masai
tongues and he would talk with me. I told him I had
come to shoot meat for his people, and this I thought
was the prudent thing to say. But he stared at me
with suspicion, and I could not blame him. He had
been brought in at the point of a Lumbwa spear, and
it was still pricking his spine.

He said that his name was Suburbe and that the
boy was his brother and that they were both sons of
Labusoni their chief.

I said, "Then we will hunt together, Suburbe, and
take the meat to your father."

He did not believe.

I told my *elmorani* to give him back his sword and
bow and quiver, and I said that his brother would be
safe with my *elmorani*. He offered to curse me if I were
not speaking the truth, and I invited him to do so.
He put his sword on the ground and stepped over it
solemnly. He said *"Bairinga Kipserageta!,"* which is
May You Be Killed by a Rhinoceros. He said *Mine Mat,*
which is May You Die by Fire.

And I said may these things be so if I broke my
word.

We went out and we sighted some hartebeest.
He whispered to me to creep after him until we came

within range of his bow. But without moving forward
I shot one animal, and brought down two more before
they ran out of range, and still I had killed them at three
hundred and fifty yards. Suburbe looked at my rifle with
respect, and he politely asked me for a little meat to
take to his family. I said that he should bring them here.

The admiration went out of his face, and I argued
with him, and in the end he stepped over his sword
again and cursed me ritually and accepted my word.

It was five o'clock in the afternoon when he returned, and with him half a hundred of his people.
They came in with their heads up, as suspicious as
buffalo, the men with bows bent. I went among them
like a curate at a church bazaar, distributing my beads
and twisted wire and Americani cloth. The women
smiled first, as women will do when you give them gifts,
whatever your motive, and these were strangely handsome women, light in coloring, with regular features
and fine figures.

But the presence of my Lumbwa made them uneasy. Suburbe made this point plain while his people
were cutting up the hartebeest. He stabbed at the air
with his hands and he said that the Lumbwa and the
Masai were always attacking the Wanderobo, someone
got killed every day and it was usually a Wanderobo. If
I wished to go further into the forest it would have to
be without the Lumbwa.

As we camped together that night I insisted on my
Lumbwa becoming blood brothers of the Wanderobo,
and there was much stepping over swords and ritual
cursing, and I had to threaten the Lumbwa that I would

abandon them to the Wanderobo if they did not agree. They agreed, but I do not think they took the cursing seriously.

Labusoni must have been in his eighties when I met him. He was not a great chief, not in the greatness that Mataia and Arab Changalla had. He had perhaps two hundred warriors where they had thousands. He lived in a sapling shelter where they lived in huts and had ritual stools to sit on when they held a *shauri*. But in spirit he was as great. He held his Wanderobo together by the strength of his personality, and he was so good a businessman that in one season he traded eight hundred tusks with Arabs in German territory.

Nothing took him away from the forest. In his old age he would still get up at sunrise and go into the trees with bow and arrow and shoot himself a buck. On the evenings before an elephant hunt he was the embodiment of his tribe.

On such an evening the warriors sent their women away from the fire, for this, what they had to do, was part of the sacred life of the male. Labusoni stood by the fire, erect and scrawny in his monkey cape, and he chanted the Elephant Song which was an amalgam of fact, imagination, mythology and mysticism. It told the whole history of the Wanderobo's elephant hunts, of the courage of one warrior and the cowardice of another, the humor and the drama stabbed home in Labusoni's high, old-man's voice. He sang of the craft and the bravery of his people, and he told them that his words went beyond their ears into the forest and were heard by the Big Ones, by the bulls and the

cows and by the calves still enveloped in the wombs of
the cows. He shrewdly reminded his people of their
flat bellies and of the sweet marrow in the Big Ones'
bones. He reminded them of the ivory and the beads
and the wire and the cloth it could buy. He told them
of the great hunts in his youth, and the old men who
had shared them with him rocked with the memories,
and the young men puffed out their chests and snatched
their swords and twirled them in the firelight, until the
iron made a ribbon of light.

Labusoni called to them one by one.

"Nyunge! Your father was no coward. In my youth
he loved to run under the bellies of the Big Ones, stabbing them. Are you afraid? Are you water? Then stay
and tend the children.

"Coboli! Your father begat none but sons from
his women. If you are turned woman then go. Look
for honey in the forest. The Big Ones are not for you.

"Minyatuke! If the thought of the thunder of the
Big Ones makes your limbs tremble, go follow the honey
bird.

"Sibibi! If your finger weakens on the bow string,
if you weaken at the scream of the Big Ones when
the arrow strikes, stay fleshing and dressing with the
women.

"Suburbe, my son! For you it is enough to remember that you are the son of Labusoni who has never
failed to kill the Big Ones since he was a youth, and
who will be killing them until his body is thrown to the
hyena."

When Labusoni had finished his song his young

warriors were calling and crying in frenzy, leaping, dancing, slashing the air with their swords, apostrophiz-ing the Big Ones, until they were dragged down and bound, and lay there still kicking and screaming. I heard them long after I had gone to bed.

In the morning they were quiet, but still wild of eye. Their hands were steady after a week's abstinence from honey-beer and women. It had been an enforced abstinence. The women first hid the honey-beer, and then hid themselves if they had to. At dawn two scouts padded out on a reconnaissance and came back to re-port. It was a good report, they had sighted a great herd, and Labusoni distributed medicine of herbs and roots among the hunters.

An arch of green boughs was erected on the edge of his little village, and he led his warriors through it, their ears strained for the sharp note of Ol Toilo, the good-luck bird, and it was important to know the direc-tion from which his call came. If from behind the war-riors, they knew that all would return safely from the hunt. If it came from ahead, or to the right, or was not heard at all, then there would be a good kill, but some of the hunters would die too. If Ol Toilo's call came from the left then there would surely be a bad kill and many men would die. In this case the Wanderobo would prudently abandon the hunt.

But on the morning the scouts reported a great herd grazing on the fringes of the Rongana forest we went under the arch and heard Ol Toilo singing blithely ahead of us. And we went to the hunt with strong hearts. We found the herd and looked down at them

where they were grouped, their ears flapping, their
trunks swinging, and even at this distance of nearly
four hundred yards I could hear their stomachs rum-
bling. It was a fine herd, with great tuskers, young
bulls, cows and their calves. They were thick in the
grass, and now and then a scimitar pair of tusks would
gleam in the sun as they were raised above the hooped
spines, and a bull trumpeted gloriously.

Labusoni spent an hour placing his men. The
marau, the old men, were sited in a copse of trees. The
lione, the uncircumcised boys, were sent to the right of
the herd, and the *elmorani* to the left.

Ten men remained with Labusoni, and because
even the Wanderobo will never attack elephant in the
tall grass, these ten men were sent forward to give
the elephant the scent of them and move the herd
toward the trees.

They went forward in the sunlight in the yellow
grass, growing smaller against the bulk of the herd,
and it was as if they were demonstrating how puny
man was compared with an elephant, and therefore how
much greater his courage and skill. They went on until
the grass swallowed them, and I saw only the sun-
pricked points of their spears. They went on until they
were on the fringes of the herd, and it was only when
they shouted, when they tore off their capes and waved
them, when they rattled their spears, it was only then
that the great heads of the elephants went up, their
ivory clashed and they slewed and stampeded toward
the trees.

The earth shook, the dust came up red about the

herd, and I saw their black bodies bouncing in it, a dark eddy on the plain as they moved toward the trees. They screamed, a hundred, two hundred, I could not say how many elephants, screaming, and the sound of it was terrible. They hit the forest and I saw the trees going down before them.

I ran down through the grass and climbed a tree to watch. In the wood the Wanderobo were waiting quietly as the herd smashed toward them, six-foot bows bent, three-foot arrows drawn to poison tips, left foot forward, body tense. And then the herd was upon them.

The arrows went in a volley. Just a thin volley with the whistling sound of it lost in the anger of the elephants, but it struck and turned the herd and sent it charging toward the flank, and there another cloud of arrows struck it, and from flank and center the arrows came in controlled volleys until the herd was wheeling and swirling and screaming, until the warriors moved in and split it into smaller groups, into single elephants isolated for death.

Now each warrior of the Wanderobo fought a duel of his own choosing, and the elephant he chose accepted the challenge and sought him out, charging with trunk up, swinging his head with the sweep of his tusks. The warrior would shoot an arrow into one flank, drop as the tusks swung, dart under the hanging belly, upstabbing with his sword, plunge out the other side and shoot in another arrow until the elephant began to roll drunkenly.

For an hour it went on as the air darkened with

the dust, and the sun dropped slanting bars through the dust, and it was hard to see anything but the heaving movements of the elephant, or hear anything above their agonized trumpeting. Now and then a bull or a cow went down with a scream and rolled over and became a dead elephant with all the majesty gone out of it, all the dignity and futile rage, and was nothing but a great carcass lying on its ivory and blood on its belly.

At last the herd broke through the warriors' ring, and got away into the open country at a gallop, their rumps swinging, tails twitching, until the grass hid them. But they left behind them nine dead elephants, and I saw the runners streaming away from the kill to call the women.

My reflexes began to work. I went down into the dust, where great trees lay broken and the Wanderobo were dancing and singing, and I found Labusoni where he was leaning on his bloodied sword. He was so thin I could see his heart moving beneath his ribs. When, I asked him, would he do something about the wounded elephants that had escaped the ring, that had gone out there in the sun and the grass to die of the poison in them?

He looked at me proudly. He said "Today we eat. Tomorrow you shall see."

The women and the children and the old people came and the Wanderobo ate where the elephants lay. They cut their way into the rib-cages with knife and axe and sword and they camped there in the bloody rooms they made, gorging the raw flesh. They staggered from one elephant to another, carrying the red, coarse-grained meat in their arms, their faces greasy, their eyes bloodshot. And the children crawled on their hands and knees through the red doors made by their fathers' slashing swords.

The great, marrowless, porous, fat-exuding leg bones were cut out, and the Wanderobo sucked them like sugar canes. They beat their way into the creamy stores of fat behind the central dome of the skull and they scooped it out with their hands. With the piercing of the abdominal wall, high up on an elephant's side, the entrails came out like the blossoming of a great opalescent flower, flowing and growing in pastel tints of appalling beauty, until the whole mass quivered five or six feet above the carcass.

I had seen hyenas and I had seen vultures tearing at carrion, and this I had accepted and even watched. But I could not watch the Wanderobo at their kill for long.

The next day they lay about their fires with stomachs distended and eyes glazed, and I could persuade none of them to join me in pursuit of the wounded elephants. On the following morning they staggered to their feet, took their bows and swords and came.

The herd had beaten an angry road from the forest into the grass, and it was easy to track. We came upon the dead where they lay, with tiny arrows held in their flanks or their bellies, and the flies on the wounds, and the vultures hanging above on the boards of their wings.

There were twenty-one elephants lying dead on the plains, and the Wanderobo swung their swords and sang.

Ol Toilo had prophesied well. It had been a great kill. Even Labusoni admitted that in his youth he had not seen such a great kill, and this admission pleased his young men. But, as Ol Toilo had promised, there had been casualties. Two warriors had been trampled to death in the forest battle, and a tusk had ripped another open from groin to chin and he too was dying.

That was my first elephant hunt with Labusoni and the Wanderobo, and when it was over, I knew that I would be blamed. Labusoni's warriors had slaughtered thirty, and when the word got around of this great kill, the Government would not stop to think that perhaps the Wanderobo would have gone hunting with or without me.

So I went up north of the line and did some hunting quietly, for eland and impala in the brown and bleak Rift Valley until the slaughter was forgotten.

Among my friends the Wanderobo was a young warrior who was the greatest hunter and the greatest killer of elephants I have ever known. With only his soft iron sword this Gabilliot, who was so called because of his light skin, could kill two rhino in one morning.

At sunrise he would start at the call of Ol Toilo to do his killing, and one morning he came upon six elephants bathing in a pool held by a saucer of hills. They were there in a natural trap, taking up the red water in their trunks and blowing it at each other, and trumpeting and splashing.

Gabilliot was a little man and stood no higher than the forelegs of an elephant, and he crawled down in the grass to that pool and watched the elephants. He watched and then he shot his poisoned arrows as quickly as he could string them, until his quiver was empty.

Each of these six elephants had three arrows driven hard into them before they realized that Gabilliot was there. They threshed in the water of the pool, their trunks up, trying to scent him, and Gabilliot lay flat on the ground with the wind in his favor, until an old bull heaved itself out of the water and found him. Then Gabilliot stood up, swinging his sword lightly, and as the elephant charged Gabilliot dodged and slashed and cut through the trunk, severing the end. He danced there, a superb swordsman, slashing until the bull turned in agony and splashed through the water.

Gabilliot waited patiently, and watched the brutes struggling up the hill. The poison was fresh, and one by one they dropped and died before they reached the top of the saucer, and Gabilliot cut off their tails and took them back in triumph to his people.

Of such strength and skill were the Wanderobo, and when the time came for me to leave them, Labusoni called his warriors together and he told them and he told me that from that day until our death his warriors were my warriors. This gift I valued as highly as the gift of one thousand *elmorani* which Mataia of the Lumbwa had made me.

Because I was now his brother, Labusoni told me of the matters that troubled him. He said that there was a medicine man called Koydelot, who was not a true Wanderobo but a Masai who had left or been driven from his *munyata,* and who had come to the forest and seduced a hundred or so of Labusoni's people from their loyalty. Koydelot had formed a colony inside the German border and there he was gathering many sheep by bartering ivory and rhino horns with Arab traders.

I decided to visit this village of Koydelot and I asked Suburbe to come with me, and I had only to ask once.

We went eastward across a beautiful plain that few white men had then seen, and there was much game there on the yellow grass, kudu in black and gray with fine spiral horns, impala and eland and antelope, guinea fowl drumming in the dongas.

We came upon the tracks of Koydelot's band, by a stream that broke the plain, where the trees were spaced out like an orchard in the Cotswolds. There was no wind to move the grass, and the water of the stream was smooth and clear, and the sand on its bed pure. On either bank the boulders were studded with mica that glistened like diamonds in the sun. We camped and washed the dust from us, and we stayed there for two days, reluctant to leave it.

On a hunt for meat on the second day I sighted lions. One came out of the grass fifty yards away and curled his lip at me. I sat on a rock and watched him, with the stock of my rifle below my right armpit, and the barrel forward across my knees. I do not think there could ever have been a safari in that country, or at least none to these lion's knowledge, for he snarled at me casually and did nothing. As he did so more lions came out of the scrub until there were twenty of them in a half moon, cubs as well.

They lost interest in me, and they lay down in the sun and yawned and scratched themselves, and I called my boy to me softly, telling him to go back to the camp for my camera. Then, because this is the way things happen, a young black-mane got to his feet and came up toward me, his head stretched on his neck and his ears back and his throat throbbing in a snarl. A lioness followed him. He came on and I had to shoot him. I had to shoot the lioness too, as she crouched to spring, and I had not wanted to shoot either of them.

There I was by the rock, alone, with two lions dead, and the others getting up out of the grass, smelling death, puzzled by the noise of my gun.

They stood there, and they switched their tails, and went back into the grass.

That night I sat with my boys about the fire, and listened to them as they boasted of their skill and courage. Suddenly they leaped up, seized their swords and went off into the darkness silently. I thought they had heard a lion, or a hyena, and had gone off in bravado to prove their boasting, because of my two lions that day, but they came back with two trembling Wanderobo who were part of Koydelot's band.

They were dragged in and my *elmorani* stripped them of their bows, their swords, their pouches of

honey, and pushed them into the firelight. But I had
their property returned to them, which was perhaps un-
wise, for as soon as they had their swords in their hands
again they swung them in an arc and jumped for the
darkness. Suburbe hit them both on the kneecaps with
his club, and they howled and sat down holding their
legs. When they saw Suburbe they seemed relieved,
and chattered to him in their bastard language.

I left them gossiping and went to bed.

At dawn Suburbe told me that Koydelot's camp
was less than two miles along the stream, and that it
had two milking cows. We went off toward it with the
prisoners, and when we got to the camp the pariah dogs
came out in a yapping wave, and I had to lay out two
of them with my club or we would never have passed
through them. Then I had to knock down their owner
who was indignantly fitting an arrow to his string.

It was a bad start, but Suburbe talked the man
out of murder.

It was a dirty camp. Koydelot came shuffling from
his crude hut, hung about with charms, a depraved
Masai, looking at me with no pleasure and asking me
what I wanted. I said I wanted milk, and I said I would
trade some sheep, which he agreed to at three rupees
each, which was shameless profiteering, for the Germans had set the price at one rupee. I did not mind
that, what worried me was the speed with which the
dirty old ruffian made friends with Kosertine, my cook
boy.

Kosertine's dinner that evening was soup and kidneys on toast. The soup was excellent, but I lost my

appetite for the kidneys, and I still do not know why. There was an old crone and her daughter sitting beyond my fire, and their ribs were showing and their arms were like canes. I called to them and I gave them the kidneys which they ate like animals. They got up with grease on their faces, and they walked five yards and fell on their faces.

My *elmorani* sprang up with their spears. I called them to me and I took my rifle and ran down toward Koydelot's camp. But he had gone, he and his people had gone in a great hurry, for their livestock was still there.

We buried the woman and her daughter and I called for Kosertine, but he had gone too. At dawn we set off after Koydelot. His people tried every trick to cover their spoor, but my trackers were Wanderobo too and could not be tricked. At four o'clock in the afternoon we came upon fresh spoor, and I knew that Koydelot could not be more than a few hundred yards ahead, and that he and his people had grown overconfident.

I sent Suburbe forward and he came back to say that the renegades were sitting in the sun eating wild plum, and sleeping. We surrounded them and came in upon them from all sides.

They sat up with their mouths open until one ran to a tree and climbed it, and sent down an arrow or two into the dust. But one of my Wanderobo strung his bow and shot back and hit this marksman in the neck. He was dead when he struck the ground.

I grabbed Koydelot by the neck and I rubbed his face in the dust until his nose bled. And I shook him

and I told him that I would take him back to Labusoni
and let the old chief punish him.

But this shows you how predictable Africa is. When
I went back to the Wanderobo, months later, Koydelot
was living among Labusoni's people and was much hon-
ored there. His medicine must have been very strong
for Labusoni respected him, and Koydelot seemed to
have forgotten the bloody nose I gave him, for he
grinned at me, and every morning shook his stones
from his calabash to see how the hunting would go
for me that day.

✳ F O U R ✳

Go to Sleep When They Roar

The lion has always had a good press agent, said Jordan.

Yet the warrior tribes thought nothing of spearing him, and some who would face a lion alone would not face a buffalo. A lion will run from you like a dog if you shout at him and there is no hunger or bitterness in him. It is when he is old and cunning, and too slow to pull down a zebra or a buck, and the hair of his mane has grown gray, it is then that he may be dangerous and will take the fight to you without invitation. For when he is old he must find his meat with the minimum of effort, where a native has been thrown into the bush after death, or where a fool sleeps without a fire.

But he is magnificent in movement, and it is this magnificence that leads people to call him King, a title which rightly belongs to the elephant. The sun ripples on his flanks as he pads through the grass, velvet upper lip lifted in a snarl, his back as flat as a table. Then he is majestic, it is true, with a regal contempt for you unless you offend him. I came upon three one day, and all I had with me was a skinning knife. I stood there with them in front of me, and I called for my rifle and hoped that someone had heard me, which

49

someone had not. But these lions watched me curiously and without malice, as a curious dog might, and finally they turned and trotted away. I know they are cats, but always they reminded me of dogs.

Lions work together. They kill as if they had a strategist among them. A lioness will drop in the grass and lie there without moving, while the males go out in a wide silent sweep, driving the placid zebra toward her until she can bring one down, and when she brings one down the others turn and run back upon the beating males to die.

Once I shot a lioness and wounded her. I broke a leg I think, and dusk came too soon for me to track her by the blood spoor and kill her. She lay out there in the brush and I heard her and the others roaring, and this was a comfort, for when lions roar at night you may go to sleep. It is when they are quiet and you know they are there, it is then that you may worry.

I went out in the morning and followed the blood and I found a strange thing. I found where she had lain all night, and all around her the grass had been beaten down by the circle of guarding males. She had arisen with them at dawn and gone off with them, and I followed the trail of a dozen lions to the river where they had taken her.

There they had left her, knowing she was dying and could not follow. She was lying by the water when I found her, and when she heard me her head came up bravely. There was blood on her flanks, and on the dragging trail she had made down to the water, but her head came up in that challenge and I saw the claws unsheathing from her pads. I shot her cleanly and the bullet killed her, which was the best I could do in my admiration.

No lion ever came close enough to claw me, and in this I was just lucky, for you can never say for sure what you would do. Geoffrey Buxton would not have believed that he would do what he did. He was out one morning with a Somali *shikari*, on the Theika south of Mount Kenya, and he was lucky to have a Somali with him for these are loyal and brave men. Buxton was carrying a double-barreled .577 and its stock, where it had been trampled on by an elephant, was bound with tape. His *shikari* carried a Mauser, and I mention these weapons because they are relevant.

They had been away from their camp for thirty minutes when they raised a handsome black-mane, and it loped away from them leisurely, having no quarrel with them. Buxton ran after it, and winded himself as he stumbled, and his breathing was hard, his eyes misted, so that his first shot was a fluke in its success. He hit the lion inside the front shoulder from fifty yards, as it turned to warn him with a roar. The bullet passed through the lion from end to end and dropped it. Buxton should have left it there and it would have been dead within a quarter of an hour, but he was not sure how badly it had been hit and he was afraid to lose it.

He came up and fired again, and this time there was no fluke and he missed. The lion rose up and charged. With a channel ranging the length of its body where the bullet had gone, the lion still had the strength to charge. Buxton put a spare shell into the chamber of his gun and as he did so he saw that the last two shots had loosened the stock, so he fired from the hip as the lion leaped, and he missed.

As they came together Buxton thrust the gun as a man might with a spear, forcing the barrel down the throat of the lion, and the animal took it in its jaws as it might a branch. Two claws went into Buxton's forearm, six inches above the hand that held the gun. They went in and through to the other side. With his free hand Buxton held the lion's mane, with his other he forced the gun further into the lion's throat.

They fell over, and the lion clawed with its hind paws as a cat does with a ball, and it slit open Buxton's thighs and calves, and only the gun in the lion's throat kept its jaws from him.

The Somali tried to fire the Mauser, but the safety catch was on, and this he did not know, or did not know how to release it. He dropped the gun and climbed on the lion's back, hitting it with his fists, gouging at its eyes, until the three of them rolled over and the lion tore its claws from Buxton's arm. He crawled away, and he picked up the Mauser and emptied it into the lion's skull.

That was a lion! Already dying, and it could fight like this.

To such men as Buxton the lion was a challenge on foot, the killing of it the fulfilment of some instinctive and savage urge. So it was too, I imagine, with Lucas, who shared a farm along the Athi with his partner Gibbons. They jumped a lion while riding along the tall river grass one morning, and raced after it. The lion went into the grass with a sudden swerve and as Gibbons' pony went by, the lion sprang. It put its right forepaw into the pony, its left into Gibbons' thigh. It held itself there and clawed at the pony's rump with its hind claws. Gibbons could not get his gun to bear on the lion, and then pony, lion and man went down.

Lucas was afraid to shoot from the saddle, so he jumped off and ran forward, and then the lion turned on him in a spring and took him down. Gibbons crawled from beneath the kicking pony and killed the lion.

They got Lucas to Nairobi hospital and the doctors looked at him and said they would have been far happier had they seen him earlier, for the poison from the lion's claws had taken hold of Lucas's legs, and if he wished to live, it would have to be without those legs. Lucas thought about this, and what it would be like in Africa for him without his legs, and he decided calmly that he would die instead. He lay in the hospital for two more days while the poison went up slowly from his thighs to his body, and he asked the doctors if there would be another day for him, and they said there would not. So he called for his friends, and they came in and sat with him drinking whisky and soda, and they toasted him a happy death and he toasted them a long life, and he was dead before dawn.

There was the lion, too, that took a man from a carriage on the old narrow-gauge Uganda Railway. This man was Ryall, the Superintendent of the Railway

Police. He and two friends had come up from Mombasa to kill a man-eater that had killed many workmen on the line between Kiu and Sultan Hamud.

The carriage was left on the siding during the night, and Ryall was in a compartment with an Italian called Parenti, who told the story afterward, but never easily because he would weep when he told it. He said he awoke during the night and found himself on the floor with something heavy and foul-smelling treading on him. He heard the crunch of its jaws and a cry, a very short and sad cry from Ryall, and then the lion was gone through the loose slats of the window.

There were many man-eaters along that railway, and they would come in groups, which is rare among man-eaters. At one time they had a station under siege, and twenty of them were shot from the doors and from the windows, and from the top of the water tank. The Hindu stationmaster sent for help, and ten askaris were sent up to guard the station, but two days later the Hindu's unhappy report came down the wire to Mombasa: *At time of roaring policemen are not so brave. Please arrange quick.*

I did my most satisfying killing of lions when I was hunting along the Anglo-German border. I was looking for buffalo. You look for one thing; you shoot another.

I knew that country and it was a country I loved. I felt that I owned it, a beautiful stretch from Victoria Nyanza to Kilimanjaro, and I made it my own particular hunting ground. Sometimes it rolled in gentle waves of short-grassed meadows, with tall, lone trees standing sentinel over bush-filled dongas. Then there would be elephant grass twice my height, splashed with shrubs whose lilac-tinted flowers were as breathlessly pure as rhododendron blossoms. There were marshes with swaying cat's tails, and great dry gullies of mud that the elephant had trampled into incredible formations. There were glades in the grass where the buffalo had made their dormitories, and tunnels padded out by rhino.

I traded ivory and rhino horn for cattle across the German border, and I sold the cattle to European settlers. I had three or four Arab agents buying cattle for me in German East and I was happy. I was good in my happiness, too. I persuaded the Masai and the Lumbwa to agree to an uneasy peace. Until then they had been raiding each other's villages, stealing young girls and putting old women to the sword, and perhaps they had grown tired of it all, for the Masai sealed the armistice with a promise of forty fat sheep for every heifer I brought to their *munyatas*.

I went from there to the Lumbwa highlands and although this was where I did my most satisfying lion-killing, the story I want to tell you has nothing to do with lions, but it was there along the Maggori River that this thing happened.

I found the river in flood, and I pitched camp and wandered upstream looking for a big tree we could drop across to make a bridge. I found another place

where the pack donkeys could swim across, and, content with myself, I sat down and filled a pipe.

I had an hour making dreams out of pipe smoke
when Masoni, my Lumbwa gunbearer, came up shaking. He said that he and the other boys had gone up
to fell the tree and found a strange animal sleeping on
the bank. They described it and I did not believe them.
From what they said it was something between a snake
and a crocodile and a leopard, which was an interesting
mutation but hardly convincing.

I sent them back up the river to see if it were still
there, and they were to send a runner back to me if
they found it again. Half an hour later Masoni came
back to say the animal was still there, but now it was
fully-exposed on the water in mid-stream. I picked up
a .303 and went back with him. I found my boys hanging from the trees, jabbing their fingers down to the
river and shaking their heads. I slid down the bank and
got in the cover of the bushes. There *it* was.

It was in midstream, about thirty feet from me, a
beast-fish, a creature from your nightmares. It was fifteen to eighteen feet in length, with a massive head,
not a head like a crocodile's, but flat-skulled and round.
It had two yellow fangs dropping from its upper jaw,
and its back was as broad as a hippo's, but it was scaled
in beautifully overlapping plates, as smooth and as
intricate as those I've seen on an old Arabian cuirass.
The sunlight fell on those wet scales and was dappled
by the leaves, and made them seem as brilliantly colored
as a leopard's coat. It had something of every animal in
it. It was impossible.

There was a broad tail, and this was swinging gently against the current, keeping it midstream, keeping it stationary, whatever it was.

At last I took aim on it. Where to hit an animal you had never seen before? For all I knew it was armoured like a rhino. I aimed the .303 at the base of the neck and gave it one solid round.

I saw the bullet hit, and heard it hit the way you do at short range. The beast turned in a great flurry of yellow water until it was facing the bank and my cover. It leaped into the air until it was standing, or so it seemed, its pale belly scales livid, ten or twelve feet on end.

I ran. My Lumbwa boys were already crashing away through the forest with me stumbling after them. We ran three hundred yards before we halted, badly blown, looking at each other. I regained my nerve at last and bullied the boys back to the river. It had gone, but its spoor was all over the soft mud, huge prints about the size of a hippo's, but clawed.

Some Wanderobo told me that they knew about this thing, they called it a *dingonek*. The Kavirondo knew of it too. They had seen more than one of them and made a god out of it whom they called "Luquata." They were worried when they heard that a white man had shot at Lukuata. They said that now they would all die of sleeping sickness, and it is true that there was an epidemic of it among the Kavirondo that year.

The current was too strong for us to build a bridge across the Maggori and we were forced to camp where

we were, and live on meat and honey as our supplies
ran out. The lions became a nuisance. They were thick
along the river and we found fresh spoor in the mud
every morning.

Ammunition was running short, too, and I re-
stricted myself to only five cartridges when I went out
to shoot meat. I argued that if I carried more, I would
waste them; and if I couldn't get a buck in five shots, I
might as well not try.

Usually I was lucky, like the day I got two topi
hartebeest with two shots. I left the porters to skin the
animals. My leg was bad with the old bullet wound and
with eczema and I got on my donkey to go back to
camp. A boy called Martinit was with me as my gunbearer.

About five o'clock we struck a bad patch of bush
and fifty yards or so from it I got the strong, acrid scent
of lion. It is a warm scent and unpleasant to the taste. I
got off the donkey and gave the reins to Martinit, took
my gun from him, and we circled the bush. We had
made a half circuit when we saw the lioness, back on
her haunches, her body quivering in those little back-
ward-forward movements as she judged the length of
her spring.

She had scented the donkey, not us, but when she
saw us she straightened up and sneered, and you could
see her making up her mind whether to spring or to
leave us. And I was thinking about my cartridges. Five
of them, two gone on the hartebeest, and I did not know
whether there was one in the breech of the gun or not.
In such cases there is only one sensible thing to do. I

pulled back the bolt, and with its action the round came back and was spun out by the ejector. It went over into the long grass, and with the lioness still making up her mind, and likely to make it up any second, there was no time for me to go searching for the lost shell. I rammed the bolt home and put one of the two remaining rounds into the breech.

The slide and the snap of the bolt decided the lioness. She turned and loped for the bush, and I should have let her go, but there was the chance of a glancing shot, and like a fool I took it.

The bullet struck her on the shoulder and she turned to charge me.

I pushed the last round into the breech and knelt for another shot, at the same time feeling in the grass for the ejected round.

She bounded toward me, but you cannot be sure with lions. A buffalo would have gone straight into that charge and nothing would have stopped it, but that lioness halted suddenly and roared. Then she turned with a whisk of her tail and ran for the bush. Recklessly I gave her the last bullet in the rump as she hit the scrub.

I began to search for the lost round, shouting for Martinit, wherever he was, to come and help me.

"Here, Bwana!" He was in a tree and shaking it with his fear.

"Get down out of there!"

He came down slowly, and I do not blame him. There was a twice-wounded lioness in the bush and I had an empty gun.

"Where the hell is the donkey?"

"Donkey gone, Bwana." He seemed to think that the donkey had had the right idea from the beginning.

I boxed his ears. It had no effect on him. I boxed them again, and he stood gaping over my shoulder to the bush. So interesting did he find that bush that I turned myself, and there was a handsome lion watching us curiously, tail swinging. Then, and I swear to this, the bushes moved all round us until there was a pride of eighteen standing there.

They became less interested in us than annoyed with each other, and began to snarl and paw. I took Martinit's arm and we soft-footed away from there until we could run to the camp.

The lions came up to the firelight that night and I kept two boys awake all night throwing brushwood on the fire, and at times I awoke and saw them in their blankets, the flames ruddy on their skins and their spear blades. I got up in the morning with the thought of that wounded lioness and I knew that I must find her and kill her. I took Martinit and half a dozen of the *elmorani* back to where I had shot her. We followed her blood spoor to a stream where she had drunk and across to the other side into the brush. I don't like following wounded lion into thick bush, and I have never heard of anyone who did. Everything is against you, and the only justification you have is that what you wound you must eventually kill, and there is a bitter irony in the fact that once you have wounded it, your animal goes to the one place where the odds are in its favor. It goes where you

cannot see it but where it can see you, and it waits to
kill you. Your rifle sweats in your hand, the flies stick to
the back of your neck, and you are very afraid. You can
tell by the footfall of your boys that they are afraid, too.
The monkeys chatter at you and tease your nerves, the
birds come up suddenly from the ground, and your arm
gets tired of swinging the rifle to your shoulder, and you
think, if you are fool enough to think at all, of the men
you knew who were killed doing just what you are doing.

My Lumbwa were ahead and behind me, long-
bladed spears poised in the right hand, shields before
them to take the weight of the lioness if she charged.
They were beautiful. They moved slowly, and with every step their heads swung from side to side, and sometimes they would stop altogether, and when one stopped
we all stopped.

The brush broke into tall, coarse grass, the tops of
it dipping over and shuddering in the slight wind. Had I
been alone I would have circled the grass and tried to
pick up the spoor on the other side, although I knew
that if the lioness had gone to ground this would be
where she would hide. My *elmorani* expected me to go
in, however, and I signaled them to follow me.

I went in ten yards, with the grass closing behind
me, and then I fell into a masked gully. As I fell I
dropped the rifle. The grass cut my palms as I snatched
at it, but this I only discovered later; what I knew then
was the scent of lion, strong, rank, as if her body were
beside me. I got on my knees and was knocked flat again

as Masoni fell on me. Now he was no longer a lion-killer but a frightened man whose spear and shield had gone the way my rifle had gone, and he smelt lion too, and he yelled, a high yip of surprise and fear that brought the other Lumbwa to the edge of the gully, chattering as they smelt lion too.

They leaped in and beat down the grass with their shields, yelling at the lioness, and when they had gone the length of the gully they found her. She was dead, and the maggots were already in her.

But we were not finished with lions on that hunt. About three o'clock that afternoon I was stretched out under the fly of my tent, watching the heat shuddering on the horizon, when the boy who was supposed to be herding the cattle came in to say that he had lost them. He said it with a great deal of shame and many apologies. I sent some of the Lumbwa to search for the cattle, and told them that while they were looking, they might find the donkey that Martinit had lost.

I was having tea, and cursing the pain in my leg, which had not been improved by the fall into the donga, when Masoni padded into camp in that lazy foot-flapping run of the Lumbwa. Bwana had best come with the rifle. The cattle trail had been found, and written all over it was the fresh spoor of lion.

I went out and came up with the *elmorani* where they were squatting by the trail. From the running of the spoor it was plain that the cattle had been in flight with the lions after them. I took the herder by the ear and tugged the truth out of him. He had been asleep when the lions came up, and their coughing had awak-

ened him and he had run. My lion-killing Lumbwa
sneered at him.

I sent back for another rifle and all the warriors
that could be spared, and we set off on the spoor. By
dusk we were more than six miles from camp, on broken,
cruel ground. So we lit a fire and sat about it, the *elmorani* with their shields leaning against their shoulders,
their spears held in their right hands, and their clacking
tongues working out the logic of the missing herd. They
said that in truth the cattle were making for their own
country, led by an old cow. They said the cattle would
follow this old cow anywhere. They were very proud of
her sagacity. I could have shot her.

I nearly did. By nine o'clock lions were roaring
from half a dozen points beyond the rim of the firelight,
and the *elmorani* drew in closer and threw more brush
on the fire, and talked a little less of the wise old cow.
The roaring went on until we heard something plunging
toward us.

We jumped up and I swung round, aiming at the
noise. It came out of the darkness suddenly. It came into
the light and paused long enough for us to see that it
was the cow. Then she passed through us and when she
saw that she was going back into the darkness she
turned and came back. The Lumbwa formed a line, and
when she reached them a second time one of the *elmorani* grabbed her humped neck. He was a brave man,
for it does not do to grab a frightened cow in the half-
light, particularly a cow that has been frightened by
lions. She fought him, bucking, tossing, and he swung
from her neck while his friends danced around them

both, soothing her with cries and encouraging him with shouts, until at last she was still, and they staked her near the fire.

All night we heard the rest of the herd crashing in the bush as the lions roared, and we did not sleep, waiting for them to come in and over us. At dawn we began to search for them.

We found ten heifers, and one of them was bleeding on the rump where a lion had misjudged its spring. By ten o'clock we had found all except two heifers and a bull, and when we saw vultures dropping from the sky a mile away we knew what had happened to these three missing persons.

When we got back to camp a Lumbwa came out to meet us. He was bleeding from the shoulders and arms, but on his face was that smirk you see on the faces of men who are well satisfied with themselves. He had seen those vultures, too, and lest we get all the glory, he had gone out and found a young lion feeding on the donkey. (So that's what happened to the donkey.) He stood up and stamped his foot and called "*Ha!*" But the lion, who put first things first, went on eating. So the *elmoran* drew back his spear arm and shot the blade. It slashed the flank of the lion which, still putting first things first, now went into a charge.

The Lumbwa took it on his hide shield, going back and over, with his sword stabbing, and the lion's claws at his shoulders, until the lion was dead with the soft iron inside him, and the *elmoran* had done no more than his people would expect of a warrior.

The main difference between a lion and a leopard is that the leopard can climb a tree. I know there are other differences, but he can climb a tree, which means that there is nowhere you can escape from him. He is the most dangerous of the cats, and therefore there is more credit in facing him and killing him, if it is credit you want.

He is a snake on four legs, and a very beautiful snake. He is cunning. He knows where to strike a man. A lion claws and bites like a bully, but a leopard springs for the head of man, which shows his wisdom. He is valiant yet he lives on dogs, and having taken one from a village will come again and again until there are no more dogs. He lives on pigs and sheep and goats, this leopard, for he has a taste for sweet meat. He kills baboons and small monkeys. He is valiant, yet he wants as little trouble from his kill as possible. Having killed he is a fastidious and methodical diner. He drinks the blood, eats the tender parts, and hides the remainder in the fork of a tree for future pleasure.

Leopards will hunt in pairs, but more often stalk alone. There is no group noun for leopards, no pride of them, but if there were one you might make it a slink of leopards. So beautiful are they in movement, so rhythmically composed that they seem boneless. They are not like lions who lie at their kill indifferent to sycophantic dogs and hyenas. The leopard has no audience when he eats, for he is inclined to turn onlookers into the next course. He'll mix with no other animals except sometimes his cousin the cheetah, and he passes through the forest very much a thing to himself.

When he is wounded or he is hungry he is superbly indifferent to danger or death. There was a particularly cunning leopard up by Kericho during the time of the famine. The bodies of the dead, the babies left abandoned made him fat and eager for human flesh. I heard of him when someone told me that a leopard had attacked two Lumbwa women who were now in hospital, or what passed for a hospital there. I went up and talked with them.

They told me that a party of *kokos*, old women of the village, had been carrying loads to Fort Ternan on the Uganda Railway. In the heat of the day they had put down their loads and lain under the trees to rest, and while they lay there this man-eater had padded silently out of the trees and bitten a piece from one of the women, like taking a bite from an apple.

She screamed, and the others woke up and screamed, and the leopard backed and pawed and snarled, rose up and bit another woman in the face before retiring. Some men came up with their spears jumping, and they went into the trees and surrounded the leopard which would not be drawn out. So they formed themselves into a line, stamped their feet, clashed their shields and shouted their battle cry. They went forward with shield braced.

The leopard sprang and landed belly down on the shield wall. It clawed the scalp from one warrior but the others crowded round and stabbed it until it was dead.

Such stories I had heard often enough before, but I thought of the leopard, and of how many more the

famine must have brought to the district, and at this
time my curiosity was distinctly purposeful for I had not
yet shot a leopard.

A few nights later I was walking from the post
office to the store with four of my Lumbwa, when a
leopard loped across the street before us. I heard one of
the *elmorani* hiss, saw the movement as his arm went
back, and heard the spear go forward. It stopped her
from springing. It held her in the flank, but she rolled
into a black and yellow ball, spitting, taking the spear
between her teeth, bending it and pulling it free. Then
she ran toward the river. We followed her but it was
too dark.

Next morning I went after her with a shotgun, and
like a fool I went alone. I found her at the water,
crouched behind some rocks, and she was only six yards
away when I saw her. I pulled up my gun, and I could
not remember whether the only charge it held was in
the right chamber or the left. The first trigger clicked. I
squeezed the second just in time, for she was already in
the air, floating toward me, ears back, paws at my head.

The shot struck her in the face and stopped the
force of her charge. She rolled, biting the grass, her eyes
gone. But she was a brave leopard. There was still the
mark of the spear on her flank. She was blind. She was
bleeding black on her muzzle, but she fought for life. I
felt sick as I watched her. I wanted to kill her. I wanted
to kill her, not because I hated her but because I was
now sorry for her.

I picked up a branch and struck her on the head,
but she did not die, she clawed out at me in her dark-

ness. I threw my skinning knife at her, and the blade stuck in her with no more effect than a thorn. I saw one of my boys standing behind a tree, his eyes wide, and I shouted for him to go back for some cartridges.

She got to her feet when I called, her bloody and blinded head swinging as she tried to smell me out, but the scent of her own blood was too strong on her, and she slipped down to the river and splashed water over her head to rid herself of the blood. And while she stood there, the muddy water going carmine, my boy came back and I killed her.

I was trekking up to Fort Ternan from Kericho, and I left too late. By dusk I had reached a farm about four miles from the station. I pitched tent near a cattle kraal and went off to see the settler who owned it. He gave me a whisky morosely. He said the Nandi were in bad blood, raiding cattle, and he wouldn't be surprised to have a call from them this night, or any night. I thanked him for the whisky and the news and went back and asked my Lumbwa if they knew this about the Nandi. They did not know, but they would believe anything about the Nandi.

I was sitting outside my tent after dinner when I heard a shout and a shot from the other side of the kraal, and I picked up a revolver and ran over. Torches were flaming over the *boma* and I found the settler staring over the thorn hedge with a gun in his hand. He said his cattle guard had heard something trying to break through and called him. We waited and heard nothing more, and I went back, thinking the cattle guard should know the difference between a hyena and a Nandi *el-moran.*

I sat by my tent to finish my pipe and as I sat there my terrier began to whine. I called to him, and there was a yellow flash, one yelp from the dog and silence. I fired. I rushed out firing until the Webley was empty, hoping that the noise at least would make the leopard release the dog. I liked that terrier. I like all dogs, but that terrier I loved.

I ran after them and I fell into a stream. I sat on the grass and I cried. I hated that leopard.

In the morning I went down to the stream with two boys. From the spoor it was either a lioness or a big leopard. The track went on into open country where the earth was black and ashy from a grass fire, and the powder of it stung the nostrils. The trail went over the ash to the lip of a ravine, and I went down on my belly and crawled forward. There, about five yards below me, was six feet of handsome leopard, asleep under a tree.

I shot it with pleasure. The bullet hit with a *thwunk,* the way you can hear a bullet hit at such close range. The leopard reared up out of its sleep and clawed at the tree. I fired again, but this was bad shooting for I was angry and hateful. The second bullet smashed the leopard's spine but did not kill it. It fell back into the grass behind the tree and we heard it spitting and screaming. It was in agony, but it had killed my terrier and I did not feel about it the way I had felt about the leopard I blinded with gunshot.

We went down into the ravine at last. The leopard

could not stand, but it was going to fight us. It dragged itself forward, hind quarters sprawled, smearing its blood on the grass. I went up to it and it spat at me as I shot it through the head.

I did not look at it again. I heard my boys laughing as they skinned it, deciding who was going to ask the Bwana for the claws.

I sat down under a tree and filled my pipe, and I told myself that at least I had done something for the terrier, which was a sentimental thought but none the less sincere. Something hit my hand lightly. It was wet and it was red and it was blood. I looked up into the tree and saw what was left of my dog, held in a fork.

I got it down and I buried it carefully in an ant hole. I put a cairn of stones over the hole to keep the hyenas away.

✳ F I V E ✳

Slayer of the Devil-Lion

I was in the Mongorrori country, said Jordan, just inside the frontier of German East. The Mongorrori were a pleasant, peaceable people with an agricultural economy that depended on the uncomplaining labor of their women. They were shorter than the Lumbwa or the Masai, more Negroid, less arrogant, but they could use spear and shield when there was need. They had the sort of hospitality and undemanding friendliness you find among people who have become reconciled to being second-rate.

I was buying cattle among them when I heard about the man-eater. I came to one of their villages and Korkosch, the head man, stood waiting in the dust to greet me, wearing his finest red blanket. He was always pleasant, but that day his cordiality was extreme enough to be obsequious, and behind it I could sense a fear of offending me. He offered me the use of one of his own huts, he quartered my *elmorani* in two others, and he told his women to bring us food. They laid it before us on leaves: cutlets of eland, eggs, fowl, green corn, butter, beans, milk and sweet potatoes. I ate, and I thanked Korkosch gravely, and because it would have been ill-mannered and would have embarrassed him I did not let him see that I knew he wanted something.

I lit my pipe and slept after lunch, and when I awoke there was Korkosch squatting in the dust outside the hut with some of his old men. Their heads were gray above their blankets, their sad faces puckered like walnut shells. They held their spears so that the hafts stood upright from the earth. I returned their compliments, and I said that I had come to buy cattle from them.

At any other time this would have been the preamble to slow, pleasing bargaining, but now they looked away over my shoulder, and Korkosch coughed, and hawked a little, and began to speak, not about cattle but about his women. He talked about the women and he talked about a lion. He spoke in innuendoes, in suspended sentences, and I listened awhile before I cut him short and asked him what this was about a lion.

He coughed again, politely, and the shoulders of his old men moved expectantly.

He said, "Nearly a moon has gone, Bwana, since the first was taken. It happened thus: Our women had gone to the fields to plant maize. They heard the screams of one of the maidens at the edge of the field, but because they were bent over their work they had seen nothing of what had happened to the girl."

The old men moaned, and I said, "And what had happened?"

"She had vanished, Bwana, and fresh in the soil were the pad marks of a lion."

I nodded.

"Then, Bwana, they came back to the village crying out, and the young men thought that the Masai
were upon us, to raid our cattle and steal our women,
and they came out with their spears. We went to the
field and there was the spoor for us all to read, and
where the lion had dragged the woman's body into the
bush. But because the trail went to the border and
across into the Bwana's country, we went no further. It
is forbidden to cross the line, and the hand of the German is heavy, and we thought: Of what use is it to bring
punishment to save a woman already dead? That night
we called to her loudly so that her spirit might hear and
be comforted."

I said, "That was well done. But what of the lion?"

He said, "The next day the women insisted that the
warriors guard them at their work, and the young men
answered angrily and would have driven the women to
the fields. But women are women, Bwana, and have
their own ways of making men do as they wish, so the
young men went to the fields with them. It is true that
nothing was heard from the lion that day, so next day
the women went to work alone."

I said, "And the lion took another of them?"

He said, "That is true, Bwana. Just after midday the
women returned weeping. They said that the lion had
taken a girl as she was gathering sticks for the fire. They
had seen no lion and heard no scream, so the Bwana will
see how quickly the lion took the girl. I ordered the
drums to sound and I called a *shauri,* a council of the
old men. We decided what to do and we sent the young
warriors out to surround the bush and drive the lion on

to their spears. They found nothing but the spoor where the lion had passed.

"The old men laughed, and they said that the young men had seen nothing but an old spoor, whereupon one of the warriors answered angrily that if we should find this lion we should find that it walked on two legs. He said that all the village knew that this second woman's husband was old, and that she was beautiful, and that a young warrior of the Sukame country had won her heart. She and this lion on two legs had run away together."

I said, "But this was not so?"

He said, "It was not so, Bwana. The next day yet another woman was taken, and this one was old and bent and there could be no young warrior from the Sukame country interested in her. We saw now that this was a matter for great thought, so I called another *shauri* to decide how to slay this eater of women. The *shauri* lasted for six days. During those six days three more women were taken."

I said, "Why did you talk so long in the *shauri?*"

He said, "That is a good question, Bwana, but the matter was not easy for us. To trap such a lion we would need to dig pits. If we set the women to dig the pits how could the fields be planted? Seed time was passing and if there were no planting there could be no harvest. This was our problem, Bwana."

I said, "But you decided on a great hunt?"

He said, "It is true. We decided on a great hunt and called upon all our warriors. For two hours the beat continued, through the forest to the plain, and then from the center of the line there came a warrior's cry, and the others in the line closed upon it. I was there, Bwana, I saw the young men fighting with a thing that leaped and snarled. I watched as it struck the shield from one warrior, and struck another young man down. It was bleeding from a spear thrust, but this thing was a leopard, Bwana, not a lion, although it was the finest leopard I have seen.

"It turned upon me and rose up to take me by the head, but I drove my spear into it, and my young men thrust theirs too, so that it fell with the spears holding it to the ground. It has taken long to tell, Bwana, but the killing passed with the speed of a thrown spear."

I said, "So it was a leopard and not a lion that took the young women and the old women?"

He said, "That is what we thought, Bwana. Never had I seen such a battle. As well as this leopard I had killed two more were also slain by my young men. We held a great dance and we laid aside our spears. Next morning the women went to work singing, and before evening another was taken."

I was silent. The old men looked at the ground.

Korkosch said, "It was a lion, Bwana, for when we examined the spot where this woman had been taken there was the spoor of a lion of great size, and this time the *shauri* sat for three days. On the third day a young man broke up the council and told us that the lion had taken an old man who had followed the honey bird that morning. It is ill for a young man to disturb old men at their council, but he went unrebuked. We saw now that pits must be dug and traps set, and this the warriors

must do. They were very angry. They said, the spear for
the warrior, the hoe for woman. They said women must
dig, man must hunt. So I spoke to them with guile for
the snake may pass where the buffalo is halted. I told
the young men that to dig these pits was not work for
women, but the making of weapons, and this was man's
work. Much more I said to them in the same fashion
until they were eager to show their manhood and dig.
But even so I thought it wise to give the hardest digging
to those who were poorest in wives and cattle."

I said, "That was wisely done, Korkosch."

He smiled. "We set them to work while their zeal
was hot. When their hands were sore and their backs
ached they quarreled among themselves, but they dug
twenty good pits. We, the old men, built traps. Some
were wooden cages with places for bait. Others were
made of logs which, when a lion passed underneath,
would break free from the vine that held them, and
crush it. Over the pits the women wove branches and
grass until even a lion, and all but an elephant, would
believe that there was firm ground there. We piled mimosa thorn so close together about the cages that not
even a duiker could slip through."

"And thus you killed the man-eater?" I said, knowing that they had not.

He shuffled uncomfortably on his rump. "We
feasted that night, Bwana, for we believed that this lion
could not escape our cunning. But in the morning when
the warriors went out they found no lion. At one pit
was the spoor of lion and the prints of a pig. It was one
of our pigs that had fallen into the pit, and the lion had

stepped down and taken it. In one case the warriors found a hyena and their anger was so great that they cut it into many small pieces. Nor is that all, Bwana."

I said, "What more?"

He said, "That night the lion came to the village and scratched at the door of old Sanduju's hut where the old man was sleeping with his three wives. And Sanduju ordered the oldest of them to get up and drive away the dog he thought was disturbing his sleep. But when she pushed aside the door the lion came in and seized Sanduju and took him away."

Korkosch took a hand from his blanket and pointed a finger at me. He said, "Bwana, is it true that this is no lion but the spirit of a warrior we have killed, and who returns for revenge in the body of a lion?"

I thought about this, and I thought gravely, for they had brought me their finest food and expected good advice in return. I said, "No, Korkosch, this is no spirit. It is a lion, and a lion can fall to spear or bullet like any other. The spirit of a warrior would return to fight with other warriors, not to kill women and old men. He would not steal a pig. Show me this lion and I shall kill it."

The old men smiled, and Korkosch asked whether the Bwana would like to see the spoor by Sanduju's hut. I said that the Bwana would. The size of it sobered me. It was the largest I had ever seen, and there was a distinct cleft in the pad of a forepaw. I pointed to it with a grass-blade and asked Korkosch whether this mark had been seen on all the spoor. He said that this was so.

I said, "Then why did you not look for it on the leopards' pads?"

His smile went cold with shame. He said that in the excitement of the kill his warriors had forgotten. But what difference would this have made, Bwana? I said that then the Mongorrori might not have feasted so confidently and made fools of themselves. I said that then Sanduju might not have been so sure that his night visitor was a dog. Korkosch said that this was indeed true, and he looked so unhappy that I changed the subject.

The spoor showed that this was a very clever lion. He had circled the hut carefully, testing its mud walls, searching for a weak spot where he could break through. My respect for him increased. I began to regret that *leave-it-to-me-you-novices* speech the great Bwana Mkuba had made. It was too late in the day to do anything, so I asked Korkosch to have his two finest trackers ready at dawn. Then, not wishing to be the lion's next victim (that would make the Bwana with the Big Medicine a very small Bwana indeed, apart from a very dead one), I had the boys build large fires before and behind my tent, and told them to keep them high burning all night.

It was a fine dawn. A cold blue, a pink flush, and then the sudden sun, with the world awakening. The first mile of the trail was easy, until it led to a ravine where the scrub and the grass were high enough to hide a cunning lion. We entered it in extended order, my *elmorani* shouting and throwing stones, and thus we made our way to the bottom of the ravine. The ground was dry, the spoor began to thin out in the dust.

But by a rock we found what was left of old Sanduju.

Now the lion would be going fast, with no body to drag, and no appetite in him for the moment.

I have hunted with trackers from all tribes, but the two Mongorrori Korkosch had given me were among the very best. Where I could see nothing they padded on confidently as if following a road, but now and then even they had to halt, to prod among the pebbles and grass, their backs bent, their thin black legs stuck this way and that, until one would cry in high triumph, and off we went again. They read the trail plainly, in a scratch on the rocks, a breath of dust over a pebble, a half-bent grass-blade.

We climbed the opposite wall of the ravine and the trail became plainer then and led us to a clump of trees walled by thick bush. Only a madman would have followed an ordinary lion into that, let alone a man-eater. The Mongorrori had elected me their madman of the season, so I lit a pipe and stared at the trees, working it out, thinking of Sanduju's bones.

The solution was quite simple. The lion *could* have gone into the thicket and out the other side. I sent the trackers to circle the trees and discover whether the trail came out. They found that it did, so I said follow it in case the devil has doubled back in. They found no back trail so I went into the thicket full of courage, and found gray hairs on the thorns. An old sinner, this lion, not fast any more, but full of craft, and guile and cunning, and he would not be easy to kill.

We took the trail over the plain, with my warriors loping along in open order, their bodies bouncing, and the blades of their spears going up and down in the sunlight, gently thwacking the hafts against their shields. I stared ahead, watching to see the lion rise up out of the grass at the noise. A child could have followed the spoor up the rise. It was too easy, he was making no attempt to run, to hide. We went up and over a hill, passing a flat stone like an altar where one of my Lumbwa silently picked up a woman's copper armlet. Down the hill went the spoor, round the base of it, and up again to the flat stone, and the tracks now so new that when I went down on my knees I could smell lion on them.

The truth was too unpleasant to be comic, although it *was* comic. The lion was following us. If we encircled the hill once more, we would become the hunted.

We held a quick *shauri*. The Mongorrori and the Lumbwa looked grave, they leant on their spears and left the strategy to me. After all, the Bwana was the one who had said he would kill this lion. I told them that I would lie on this flat stone with my gunbearer, even as the old lion had lain and watched us. They would beat the country below and drive the eater of women out of cover where I could shoot him.

Masoni and I lay in the sun and watched them down there, their knees going up and down as they beat the grass, their shields rising and falling, and their ululating cries coming up.

I saw the lion as Masoni clutched my arm. Three hundred yards away and running swiftly. I have killed hartebeest easily at this range, but I fired twice at that lion and missed.

Eight hundred yards away he stopped, and turned, and had the impudence to lie down. I gave him another round and saw it kick up the dust far short of him. He roared at us, and went off, and the grass and the night had him then.

We went back to the village, and the Mongorrori trackers were silent. I don't think they thought much of me, or perhaps they thought all the more of a lion that could not be hit at three hundred yards. I sat late over my fire, trying to think of some means of killing this lion without a day-long trail. At last I told the boys to heap more brushwood on the fire and I went to my tent. The fires outside made the canvas ruddy with leaping shadows. I tied back the flap, and as I picked up my rifle to place it by the bed a lion coughed just beyond the firelight.

I turned with the gun, my thumb pushing forward the safety catch, and as I turned I saw the lion leaping *over* the fire, his jaws wide, his claws extended, and his mane like a ruff. He took the boy who was building up the fire. The boy screamed, and was dragged away with his legs threshing, his shoulder in the lion's jaws. He called to me.

I brought up the rifle to a steady rest against the tent pole, but before I could get the sights aligned lion and boy were fifteen yards from me, and the boy's body masked the head and flank of the animal. I sent a bullet

into the lion's rump. He dropped the boy and roared. I
aimed at his shoulder, but the second bullet hit him too
far back to drop him, and he was gone.

Women were screaming, and warriors were pad-
ding up and down clashing their spears, but none of
them went beyond the firelight. I got the boy to my tent
and poured half a flask of whisky down his throat. I
washed his shoulder and drenched it with iodine. Nobody slept that night. The Mongorrori crouched in front
of their huts, and built up the fires, and the lion roared
at us out of the valley.

At dawn I set out after him, with the Mongorrori
behind me, all of them wanting to blood their spears in
this lion. The first hundred yards of the trail showed us
plainly that my rump shot had maimed him and he was
dragging a leg. He was bleeding badly, and we found
gouts of it that he had coughed up. I thought: We'll
find him dead. He has a broken leg and a bullet in the
chest, we'll find him dead.

He had stopped to drink at a stream and there was
blood again on the pebbles and the grass. He was dying
well, this lion. We followed the spoor for another mile,
with the blood thicker, and then the trail led into the
brush and did not emerge.

The Mongorrori surrounded the scrub and began
to move in, calling, their spears ringing against their
shields. They meant to drive him out to where I stood.
If he were still alive. They shouted, and he roared back
at them. He was still alive. He roared strongly. He was
still very much alive.

I did not enjoy the thought of receiving his charge at such short range. I said, leave him. I said, "Let his leg stiffen and the blood come out of him."

This sort of talk did not match well with my boasting by the fire, and the Mongorrori ignored me. Let the Bwana kill like a warrior. They went on, clashing their spears. I stood by a tree. It was a good tree, good, I mean, because it was broad enough to slip behind. One old man stayed with me. He had scars all over his body from spear thrusts and claw gashes, he was a relic from the old fighting days of the Mongorrori when they would have killed their own lion and not asked a white man to help them. But he was old now, and I suggested that perhaps his place should be taken by a younger warrior.

He looked at me and he said, "Bwana, my daughter was one whom this lion took." He held up the copper armlet we had found by the altar stone.

I said nothing. We stood in the shade and watched the young men moving in on the scrub. They did not go in boldly as the Masai would have gone in, but they went in, nonetheless.

The old man thumped his spear haft. He said, "Bah! The young men move like oxen. In my days we should have slain this lion twice by now."

He shortened his spear, lifted his shield and trotted calmly toward the bush, and the lion came out at him. He took its charge on his shield, his body crouched and braced, and as the lion knocked the shield aside he drove his spear into it. He did not kill it and it went

down on its side and then stood up. The old man leaped
away and looked toward me.

I was already sighted on the lion. It was a good
shot, a very good shot, and this lion owed me a good
shot. The bullet broke its spine and it fell quickly. The
old Mongorrori drew his sword, raised it to me, and
then slashed the lion across the face.

Up came the young warriors, jostling about the
body, driving their spears in, plucking them out, and
driving them in again until his old coat was bloody and
he was very, very dead. They cut off his forepaw, the
left one, and there in the pad was the cleft.

It was two days, two days of feasting and the drinking of honey-beer, before I could get the Mongorrori to
discuss a cattle-trade. Korkosch presented me with a
milch cow and a heifer. The presentation was made at
the end of a long speech in which I was referred to as
Koufiwa Simba Sitani—slayer of the devil lion.

The title would better have gone to Scarface, with
his spear and his shield and his contempt for young warriors.

In Tommy Wood's store, in the Station Hotel, the
settlers would argue their reasons why natives allowed
themselves to be killed by a lion. It was little of an argu-
ment, since they were all agreed. It was due to lack of
nerve.

But many of the warriors I knew who were killed
by a lion, or frightened by lions, were great warriors
who had slain a lion before they were out of their teens,

and few of those settlers would have faced a kudu with a spear and shield, let alone a lion. These *elmorani* were lion killers, and when they faced a lion with legs braced and shield up, there was no fear in them and no nerve to lose. A man could either kill a lion or he could not, and if he could not, then he was a woman.

But that was when they went out there to kill or be killed, and it was part of life and they accepted it. It was something quite different when the lion came upon them suddenly, and took them out of their hut, out of the firelight, then the lion was no longer a lion, it was *Simba Sitani.* Then the *elmoran* was not a warrior but an unprepared and frightened man.

Fear comes easily to all men because even the dullest of us has some imagination. I was always afraid when I stood there with gun up, waiting for a charge. But if I did anything, it was to obey certain automatic reflexes that told me not to run because it was safer to stand, that told me where to hit this animal so that it came down with one shot, that told me when to take first pressure, when to take second.

These things I did, calmly if you like, but I was not unafraid. You are always afraid after you have seen your first human being clawed by a lion or bonestripped by a buffalo. And I think it was the same with the *elmorani,* they were able to do what they did because the conflict was of their own choosing.

But having a lion or a buffalo on you suddenly, when you are not ready to fight, when you have not wound up your courage the way men do before a crisis, then that is something very different, and fear is the only thing you have in you.

So I took little part in those arguments about why the natives are so foolish as to let themselves be killed by lions.

❊ S I X ❊

The Natives Weren't Always Hostile

The natives weren't always hostile, said Jordan, and smiled.

If the Wanderobo, the little *shenzi* of the forests, were my friends, so too were the Lumbwa. My boys were always Lumbwa *elmorani*. With the Masai and the Nandi they were the peerage of the plateau country. The lands of the Lumbwa stretched south of the Uganda Railway for about eighty miles, and along it for twenty; and at Kericho, to keep the Masai and the Lumbwa and the Nandi tractable, were two British officers and a company of African Rifles, a District Commissioner and fifty police.

The Lumbwa were slender, graceful, chocolate men, with regular features and thin, straight noses; with the great gifts of laughter and honesty and the rarer virtue of loyalty. They robbed each other, stole each other's women, fought little, futile and bloody battles in which there was no strategy but the breaking of shield-wave on shield-wall. They mustered their *elmorani* in proud regiments under the insignia of the Buffalo, or

the Lion, or the Leopard, or the Rhino. To see a line of
such spearmen coming through the yellow grass was to
be the witness of a barbaric and splendid thing. The
sunlight held on a spear point until a turn of the haft
sent it running liquidly down the yard-long blade. The
leather sheen of brown skin, red-clayed hair swinging,
white-beaded gaiters coming up and going down. Naked
swords hanging from shoulder slings. Now the shields
going out, now the shields coming back body close, with
a great and thunderous *"Huw!"* of contempt and challenge. The regimental leaders proud in leopard hoods.
The dance of black and white ostrich feathers. These
were the Masai and the Lumbwa and the Nandi in their
youth.

And when they grew old they sat outside their huts
and talked of their valiant youth, and made their imagination drunk with the tobacco juice they poured into
their nostrils.

Toroni was a great chief of the Loita Masai. His
munyatas, his villages, stretched through belts of timber
in the highlands to break on the country of the Setick
Lumbwa. His *munyatas* were fortresses, and studded
the Loita Plains like the old keeps of border clans. A
thorn zareba, three hundred feet in diameter, enclosed
the long, low, round-topped, dung-plastered, thatch and
wattle huts. Into this circle at night were herded piebald
sheep, sleek humped cattle, and the gap in the zareba
was closed after them. A Masai *munyata,* a *munyata* of
the Lumbwa or the Nandi, was built for defense. Each
hut was built for defense. Its doorway did not open at
right angles to the hut, but ran inward along the wall, a

low passage, so low that an enemy would have to crawl on his hands and knees and bring himself helpless to the thrust of a spear.

The Masai, pre-eminently, were men who lived for battle, against other men or against animals, and the young boys herding cattle eagerly awaited the coming of a lion so that by killing it they could become *el-morani*. The Masai ploughed nothing, grew nothing, reaped nothing. They tapped the necks of their cattle for blood, mixed it with milk, drank it and were men on it.

They traded goats and sheep with Hindus and Arabs and Somalis, and you saw them at this trading, long arrogant men standing on one leg, holding their spears, and sneering at the Hindus, the Arabs and the Somalis.

When I first went to British East it was considered foolhardy for a white man to go down to where the Setick sept of the Lumbwa held their land, and when I went into it, some of the Lumbwa had never seen a white man, and they climbed to the roofs of their huts to see me better, while the women and children hid behind the cattle.

Warriors, their faces striped with paint, would walk up to me and stare insolently, or straddle a narrow path with spears leveled. When I walked on, as I knew I must walk on or take the spear in my back, they stepped aside with a dignity that made me feel that I was deferring to them.

My friends were Arab Changalla, chief of the Setick Lumbwa (who was not an Arab, since the word is

merely a prefix meaning *son of*), and Mataia, chief of
the Manga Lumbwa. These were not my friends as you
might make friends of your neighbors; these were my
brothers. When I first met Arab Changalla, standing in
his leopard skin before his old men, we stared at each
other for many seconds, and then we gripped hands.
We both knew instinctively that there was a deep
friendship between us. In Arab Changalla I had a friend
you could not buy with a ten-pound tin of beads or a
bolt of Americani cotton. I traded well with Arab Changalla. He never cheated me, his warriors never betrayed
me, his *munyatas* never rejected me.

Mataia's *elmorani* ranged down the Engabai plains,
and those who questioned his despotism he killed. Yet
he was a boy, he hunted like a boy, and would leave his
hunt to join my safaris. His wives were always young,
with round, shining, hairless heads. His children ran
round-bellied about his blanket fringe. A wife whose
cooking offended him would be forced to eat all of it,
pot after pot, and this followed by quarts of water until
she understood the passion of his anger. If another
stitched his cloak too clumsily he would lay a heated
sword blade across her stomach. If another looked too
lingeringly on a young *elmoran* he would slash with his
sword to mark or to kill according to the length and the
longing of her glance.

Without the friendship of Mataia and the friendship of Arab Changalla, without an intangible passport
from the Masai, I could never have traded and hunted
ivory across the Loita Plains and into German territory.
But with their friendship I did so much trade that I em-

ployed a Goanese clerk in Kericho to keep my books, and I had a house there too, wattle and daub with three large rooms, doors and windows of elephant cane, a veranda for my chair. I had a Somali cook and a houseboy. This was when I was young to Africa and thought it fine to be a property owner, as if the rest of society needed the sight of my house and my houseboys to be assured of my success.

But Africa caught my feet, and my friend Mataia knew this when he raised his spear and called, *"Hodi, eldama elmoran! Hodi, Mongaso!* Greetings, elephant warrior! Greetings, man who is always moving!"

I made so much money trading out of Kericho that I started other posts at Terna and Muronea. I made so much money that I lost interest in it, which is perhaps the best thing that can happen to a young man.

I did not feel one way or the other about the Nandi because my heart had gone out to the Lumbwa, as it was later to go out to the Wanderobo. But the Nandi were warriors like the Lumbwa or the Masai, and they had their splendid swordsmen and their regimental insignia on their buffalo shields.

The Nandi lived northwest of the railway line, on a river-drained plateau between Kisumu and Mount Elgon. They were more feared by others than the Masai, and I believe them to be greater warriors, although, like the lion, the Masai have had their press agents too.

The Nandi decided to go to war while I was trading among the Lumbwa fifty years ago, and they went to war with a shrewd idea of what should come first.

They tore down the telegraph lines, having learned the importance of these to the white men, and they made bracelets and necklaces from the copper. They took the bolts and fishplates from the railway lines, melted down the iron and fashioned the metal into spears and swords, and when this was done, and they were properly ornamented and adequately armed, they padded out in their regiments and went raiding southward.

They sent messengers to the Lumbwa inviting them to join the foray. The Lumbwa replied that they were friends to the Nandi, of course, but was this the time for war? The Nandi replied that any time was the time for war, and if the Lumbwa were women they could stay in their *munyatas* while the Nandi enjoyed themselves. So the Nandi regiments raided on their own and came further southward every day until they were burning and looting, stabbing and stealing all around Kericho.

The company of Rifles had gone up to Murhoni on the Uganda Railway, and in Kericho the DC's assistant, Ainsworth, got everybody into the fort and, looking like a beleagured garrison commander, asked for someone to go to Murhoni and inform the Rifles that the people they were looking for were in fact down south.

I found myself volunteering.

I went off in the moonlight on my own, and it was twenty-five miles to Murhoni. It was quiet and I saw no war parties until I struck the railway, four miles from the station. At that moment the moon set and I sat in the brush until dawn.

At daylight I had trekked two miles along the rails

when I saw a company of Nandi on a rise to my left. There were perhaps fifty of them, silently watching me, a ripple of brown and white, of black and red and blue, their spears slanting across their shields and the wind moving in their plumes.

I ran. I was tired. I was wearing heavy boots. But these were inconsequential handicaps. The Nandi were great runners and they could have caught me had I been barefoot and in my first wind. They flooded down the rise, slapping their shields.

I got to a bridge, with gaps between the sleepers, and the river in flood below, and I went over, jumping from sleeper to sleeper, with the Nandi after me. They called on me to stop and be killed. About a mile from Murhoni I accepted the invitation, to stop at any rate. I stopped with the breath in me hot, and I fired. They slipped into the trees and taunted me, and I knew that some of them were slipping up through the forest to outflank me.

But my firing brought the askaris from Murhoni, and with them a regiment of Masai levies who were happy to meet the Nandi. They came on at a trot, shields forward, spears up, their red hair dancing, and they went past me, with the Nandi coming out of the trees one by one and running.

There wasn't much to that little Nandi war after that. The young *elmorani* had enjoyed it. They had made at least one white man run for his life, and they finally let the old men hold a *shauri* and call off the war. They handed back some of the women they had captured, they paid a few fines in cattle, and they

closed their eyes when the *lione* stole a few more to
even the loss.

But something worse than a tribal war happened
then—famine. I have seen few things worse in Africa
than famine, perhaps sleeping sickness, but famine
makes it longer in the dying. It was bad, very bad.
Mothers left their children by the trail for the hyenas
to eat. One morning I opened my house door in Kericho
and found twenty abandoned Lumbwa children, none
of them older than eight and most of them babies, sitting in the dust with their bellies blown out and their
hands and feet ridiculously large at the end of thin
legs and arms. The flesh had gone from their faces until
you could see just the skull and their brown, melan-
choly eyes.

Hyena and leopard and lion gorged on the bodies
of children left like this to die. At night I could not
sleep. I heard the triumphant cries of these animals
as they found another child.

The famine seemed to kill Kericho. The troops
went, the Hindu shops closed and their corrugated iron
roofs rusted and fell in. I think it was then that John
Boyes went up alone among the Kikuyu to get food
for the famine area. I went down among the Setick
and shot game to feed the people of my friend Arab
Changalla.

I went searching for rubber while I stayed with
Arab Changalla, and I found it in the forests. Rubber
vines, as thick as your thigh at their base, their leaves
as flat and broad as a Zulu assegai. I went in to Nairobi

to get a concession and I ceased to be a happy hunter
and became a worried man who needed signatures to
pieces of paper. While the lawyers and the deskmen
were arranging these pieces of paper into neat, conse-
quential order, I went north. I went prospecting and
trading northward to the Eldama Ravine and the
Kamasi country, and on still further, dropping ten thousand feet into the Muty Valley where I found the peace
and beauty of God.

A thousand streams drained the highlands, and
sang through banks of moss and orchids, dropped into
black pools where the rhino and buffalo cooled themselves at noon. The air was sweet and the game was
placid. I found garnets and cat's eyes in the blue soil,
which was about the extent of my prospecting. But
since every Eden must have its serpent, I heard about
the Maraquet. Very bad people, the Maraquet, I was
told. Even the women fought with bows and poisoned
arrows.

The serpent had an apple, however, and the Maraquet had ivory, and this I was told, too, and remembered. I did not meet the Maraquet then, but I remembered the stories about them.

A year, two years later, I do not remember, I was
back in the country. My rubber-tapping scheme had
passed, as many schemes passed with me, and I was
ivory hunting again, and feeling good about it. I sold
the ivory to a Hindu storekeeper called Mohammed,
although he never had enough cash to pay me. He told
me that the Maraquet had many tusks and a man could
buy them for cattle, for hides, even for goatskins.

Mohammed told me he would pay me top prices for any ivory I brought in from the Maraquet. He told me happily that the Maraquet had recently ambushed a platoon of askaris on the Torkwell River, between Baringo and the Ravine, and had murdered them all. I looked at him, and having told me the risk, he now dangled the bait. He said that a Persian called Hadji Askar was even then preparing a safari to go ivory trading among the Maraquet. Surely the sahib would want to get there before a Persian.

I bought twenty heifers, and I bought ten donkeys at two pounds a head to carry the ivory I thought I was going to get. I hired twenty Kavirondo as porters, a cook, a gunbearer, a boy, and two Arab traders. We took blankets, iron wire, beads, calico, unbleached cotton. With the cook and the boy driving the herd, we set out on a seventy-mile trek, forty of them through the hard Muty hills. On the crest of those hills you are nearly ten thousand feet nearer to God. The Ushangish Plateau is behind you, the Elgeyo Valley ahead, and when we went down into that valley we discovered that we had arrived in the middle of a tribal war.

It was the Nandi again. Their regiments were raiding and the people of the Elgeyo were under arms. When we reached the first village we found Elgeyo warriors strutting about the huts, their bodies smeared with red clay that the rhino like to wallow in, their faces painted, their spears burnished, and their tongues clacking as they bragged of what they would do to the Nandi. They were going to have their chance, for as we came in, we had seen three or four Nandi regiments over the hill, a mile from the village.

The Elgeyo knew they were there. Our safari was ignored as the warriors shuffled around outside the village, falling into the regiments with the same dispirited disorganization you see in a European regiment before it is called on parade. Then, before the Elgeyo were ready, the Nandi appeared out of the grass on the rise, and looked down. There must have been fifteen hundred of them.

I got out my glasses and focused on them. They were magnificent. I could pick out the Buffalo Regiment and the Zebra Regiment from the insignia on the shields. They stood there, stamping the grass and crying *"Huw!"* while the wind tossed their plumes, and their long stabbing spears went up and down, and the sun shone on black arms, on iron swords.

The appearance of them brought a thousand or more Elgeyo into line, and the Nandi trotted down the slope of the hill to the level ground, and although the tactical advantage of surprise was theirs, they went over to the defensive and formed a shield wall.

In the Elgeyo village the women began to scream as they drove the cattle away eastward, toward the nearest village of their neighbors, the Muty.

Ignored by both Nandi and Elgeyo, I decided that this was a private war and no one was going to bother us so long as we minded our own business. My Kavirondo had formed themselves into a little phalanx, but I broke them up and told them to lower their spears.

Or did they think they could fight fifteen hundred
Nandi and fifteen hundred Elgeyo on their own? Yet I
put on my revolver and I tucked the stock of my
sporting .303 beneath my arm. I was in the front row
of the stalls, and I could become part of the play any
time the cast chose to make me.

The Elgeyo took the initiative. The sun was at
their backs, which shows how little of a tactician the
Nandi leader was. The Elgeyo went forward in three
lines, feet thumping, war-crying, a wall of shields going
up, tufts of lion-hair bobbing on their buttocks. Twenty-
five yards from the Nandi battle line they halted. They
threw stones, and for a moment or so it was like a boy's
game, with more courage in words than in actions. The
Nandi stopped the stones with their shields and jeered.
Sometimes an Elgeyo threw a rhino-club or a spear, and
the Nandi endured this for a while before they charged.

The two shield walls went together with a crash
and the lines broke, into little swirling groups, with
warriors crouching, striking, stabbing, until there was
little I could see but the red dust and the shine of
spears.

They were evenly matched and there was much
noise. When the Elgeyo gave ground the Nandi roared.
Then the Nandi gave ground and the Elgeyo went forward with a great triumphant grunt. There were bodies
on the ground, and others staggered out of the dust
with sword gashes on their chests and arms. And they
looked as all men look coming wounded from a battle,
as if the glory is not worth it.

My tent came under range of the spears and the

stones. I told my boys to pull it down and get under cover in the trees. They were doing this when the Elgeyo gave ground again and the flank of the Nandi came swarming over us. They drove my carriers off and one big *elmoran* came swinging at me, with his spear up and his eyes bloodshot. I could have shot him. I felt like shooting him for the impertinence. But when he was a few yards off I began to swear at him in Nandi. He stopped, grunted, and came on at me with spear again, until his chief called him off, and he went back to hit at the Elgeyo.

Small parties broke from the wings of the Nandi line, outflanked the village and set off in pursuit of the Elgeyo women and cattle. It was a foolish move, for it weakened the Nandi strength and the Elgeyo, driven back to within a hundred yards of their huts, moved forward again. And now a band of Muty came thudding through the village to help them. The Nandi war chief gave out a high, gobbling cry, and his regiments backed up the hill, paused to call obscenely, and then were gone.

It was a surprise to count only twenty dead in the grass.

After the Elgeyo had got over their celebrations they told me that the nearest Maraquet village was forty miles away. I sent on two porters to tell the Maraquet that I wished to trade with them, and while I waited I went hunting rhino for the horn. My porters came in four days later with the news that the Maraquet would be pleased to sell me their ivory, had I the courage to go and get it. It was the sort of brag that cowards make, and the Maraquet lost some stature by it.

I left most of my equipment behind, but I took the cattle, six Lumbwa and one of the Arab traders. When we reached the edge of the Maraquet country, I built a zareba and herded the cattle into it. I pitched a ground sheet in place of a tent, about a hundred yards from the nearest Maraquet village, and the Maraquet themselves came out to watch me. After the Lumbwa, the Masai and the Nandi they were unimpressive, short, ugly, and without pride. My *elmorani* went into a sulk of disgust.

A deputation came out to ask how many cattle for a tusk. I said, "How about showing me a tusk first?" They went off and came back with a small thing, not much more than twenty pounds, and I began to wonder where Mohammed had got his information. I said, "Big ivory." They said, "Two head of cattle, Bwana, and big ivory shall be brought." I looked disgusted, and to emphasize my disgust I said that I would buy goatskins instead.

At this a warrior shifted his spear and shield and offered me a skin about the size of a rabbit. I kept my temper. I think I kept my temper. But the warrior lost his. He threw the skin in my face and snatched one of my trading blankets. As he straightened up I hit him as hard as I could under the jaw, and then I beat him over the head with his own shield. This delighted his friends.

I told my boys to pack up, we would return to the Elgeyo, but an old chief hobbled out from the huts and waved his skinny arms at his people. His indignation almost convinced me, and I accepted his invitation to stay. As a token of his regret he had his women bring some goatskins which were superlatively better than the rag I had just been offered. He saw approval on my face and grinned at me from naked gums. Would the Bwana allow his warriors to examine the cattle?

They separated two heifers from the herd and went over them thoroughly with their hands, grunting their satisfaction. The chief said that in the morning much ivory would be brought in exchange for these heifers.

But at nine, in the dark, when I was lying under my netting counting the stars, Mabrukie the Arab came up whispering. He said that the two heifers that the Maraquet had chosen were dead. Poisoned thorns had been driven deep into their polls.

I sat up and looked across to the village. It was quiet, but I put a revolver under my pillow and lay down again. Mabrukie came again after the moon rose. He said that he had seen fifty spearmen slipping away from the village to the forest, and there were others awake in the village, for he had seen them moving close to the ground.

We moved out quickly. I had the boys drive the cattle from the zareba and we made good time, and I do not know now why the Maraquet did not come out of their village once they saw us moving. Instead they beat their drums and sounded horns, and if those fifty spearmen intended to ambush us they must either have lost their nerve or chosen the wrong spot, for by dawn we were back in the Muty country without seeing them.

The Muty were very unhappy about the whole affair, and I suspected that the rumor about the Maraquet being great ivory owners had started with the Muty. They sat in *shauri* and decided to help me. They said that if I gave them four heifers they would go off and trade them to a well-inclined friend of theirs among the Maraquet. I trusted them, and they returned in two days with two tusks weighing forty pounds each. And this was little enough for a man who had set off with twenty heifers, ten donkeys, twenty *elmorani,* beads, calico, blankets and cotton. That was not what you would call a successful trading expedition.

But in view of the news which the Muty also brought me I had small reason to complain.

The Persian trader, Hadji Askar, had arrived in the Maraquet country a day after we left. The Maraquet stole his cattle and drove him in a bloody spear fight all the way to the Suk country.

I hunted okapi among the Mabuti in the Belgian Congo. I had been shooting elephant and trading ivory out of the Semiliki forests and had seen what I believed to be okapi spoor now and then, a clean, darted track like an eland's. I wanted an okapi the way you want something that is rare just because it is rare, and the way you want to do something that no one else has done, for this is the vanity of all hunters. There was no danger in hunting okapi, as there is with the lion, the elephant and the buffalo. In the hunting of the okapi the credit lies in finding the animal.

So when I saw this spoor in the Semiliki forests,

the spoor that looked so much like an eland's but was not, I knew that perhaps I had found an okapi. I sent for the old men of the nearest village and I described the eland to them, but they shook their heads and said that they had never seen one. With a stick I drew the horns of an eland in the dust, and still they did not recognize it. So I knew I had seen okapi spoor, and when I found them again I sent for the old men once more and showed them. They nodded and said *"Kengi!"*

They took me back to their village and produced a skin, a beautiful skin, white on the belly, the neck and back a purple-black, the buttocks barred with black and white. This was the skin of an okapi, that gentle, douce animal so uncharitably described as half-antelope, half-giraffe.

"Where," I said, "do I find a *kengi?*" They said in the forests, deep in the forests among the Mabuti, the little people. They said no one had killed a *kengi* without the help of the Mabuti. I said, "Bring me a Mabuti who will talk to me."

Two days later they brought me three of them.

They were not beautiful. They were monkeys without fur. Little, hump-buttocked men with flat, expressionless faces, and curled beards like Spanish hidalgos. They were ageless, but they were powerful within their tiny frames, and they stank from the stale grease on them. I told my gunbearer to take them away and feed them, and ask them about the *kengi*.

In the afternoon my bearer said the Mabuti were happy now, having discovered that I wanted something which, in their opinion, only they could get for me. They offered me a skin if I shot some meat for them, elephant preferred.

I wanted to shoot my own okapi, not buy a skin, but I agreed to go on an elephant hunt in the hope that if we struck okapi spoor we could follow that as well.

The Mabuti disappointed me. I had heard, and I had believed that the pygmies were warlike, brave, great hunters. I had heard that even the biggest tusker could not frighten them. But this was not so.

For two miles into the forest the paths were strewn with fresh elephant sign. The light was a pale blue twilight, and where the sun came through the roof of the trees it fell in bars that were almost tangible. The paths were walled with bushes eight, ten feet high, broad and black-leaved like rhododendrons, but carrying great masses of lemon-yellow fruit. The air steamed and broke the focus of one's sight, and I sweated until my brown cord jacket doubled its weight.

We heard the Big One at last, the crash of branches and the rumble of his stomach. The Mabuti heard him and trembled and chattered among themselves. They said that the bull was full of devils. They said he knew that we were coming and was laughing because he would kill us all. I asked where were these brave Mabuti I had heard about, and before they could tell me, the Big One scented us. His trumpet blared and the Mabuti ran.

One ran through the legs of my bearer, upsetting him just as the bull charged into view, coming down the path like a train emerging from a tunnel.

I brought it down with three shots. The Mabuti came back, but not with haste. I could see their faces peering from the bushes at first, and then their tiny bodies emerging, until they ran out and climbed all over the Big One, strutting like peacocks as if they had killed him. I said, "Bring your families and have a feast."

The headman plucked at his beard, puffed out his belly, and said that the elephant rightly belonged to him and two or three others whose *shambas* had been destroyed by this elephant. The rest of the tribe could find their own elephant.

I said that if it came to the point the elephant belonged to the Belgians, and they had sold it to *me*. I had a piece of paper that said this. But the Mabuti were sly. They knew that all I wanted was the tusks, that was all any white man wanted.

I settled the problem by having some of my boys cut out some meat and give it to the pygmies. They went away and came back with three more of their tribe and also some women. The women were, if possible, more ugly than the men, but their naked bodies were smooth and beautiful, like exquisitely proportioned statuettes of ebony.

I still wanted my okapi, and now that the Mabuti had their elephant they had no excuse for not helping me. We moved camp twenty-five miles, and took the nomadic dwarfs with us. On the second day we saw fresh okapi spoor, and the Mabuti took it up enthusiastically. The country here was bad, and it took us all morning to struggle through three miles of swamp and underbrush, and we made too much noise to hope for a sight of the animal. I went back to camp and told my best gunbearer to take two of the Mabuti and find a pool where the okapi came regularly to drink.

They found one and I left at five the next morning, down a broad, straight avenue made by elephant through the trees. Within an hour we got to the pool. It was the saucer of a swamp, perhaps five hundred yards by eighty, with a stream curling the length of it, and red and scarlet flowers set in the green sunlight.

I put up a crude blind on the incline that gave me a clear line of fire, and I sat back on my heels biting a dry pipe, waiting. It was like watching a film, like looking at the illustrations in a smooth-papered encyclopedia where all the animals of Africa are miraculously gathered around one drinking pool. They came down from the trees and they drank, and sometimes they stood with head and body tense in suspicion before they went away.

A leopard came and the Mabuti wanted me to shoot it, but I was not shooting leopard just for their amusement, and scaring away my okapi by the shot. It was a temptation, however, the brute was so damn sure of itself. It sat at the edge of the pool and licked its chest like a cat.

Four elephants came and wallowed in the mud, and squirted the water at each other, and had great fun before they pulled themselves out and ambled away, and they were a temptation too, for one had fine tusks. I sent a pygmy back to bring some food and a camera, and he came back, and we sat on until five o'clock. Twelve hours now. It was teatime. The forest came to drink, pretty little duikers drinking daintily. A lone bull elephant with only one tusk and I photographed him while he posed. A small herd of elephant came after him, had their drink and water play, and went. But still no okapi.

Then he came.

He came in a herd of buffalo, the clever one. I tried to photograph him but he was screened by those big black brutes with their pulled-down horns and their dancer's hips. Then my gunbearer sneezed. He got his hands over his mouth but just the same he made a choked, graveyard moan in his throat. I saw the horns of the buffaloes go up, saw the herd break, and saw the okapi clearly for the first time.

He was fine. He stood about five feet at the shoulder, the same height as an eland, the black and white fetlock rings making him seem oddly unfinished about the legs. His head was cocked on his long neck, slanting his four-inch horns in their soft skin jackets, his eyes moist and alarmed.

"*Kengi!*" whispered an old Mabuti, as if seeing a vision.

Then he was away, this fine okapi. He slewed round and went with the bouncing black rumps of the buffalo. I gave him a snap shot and saw his haunches slither. I had hit him. I said I had hit him, and my bearer agreed. "*Piga!*" he said.

We went over, but the blood spoor was slight, and

it was late. Always it is late when you have this luck. I gave up the trail and worked out my impatience on the gunbearer. Him and his sneeze.

We found the trail in the morning, although some rhino had kindly walked over it in the night. We followed it and then lost it. I moved camp, but I saw no okapi again, and I was hard to live with. A week later the little people came in with a skin and offered it to me. They said they had found the okapi in one of their pits and this was the okapi we had seen at the pool. I examined it carefully but there was no bullet mark on its flanks, and I knew I had hit my okapi. But I thanked the Mabuti and I rewarded them for their trouble, and I never again did shoot an okapi.

The Kisi were an odd people. You knew where you were with the Lumbwa and the Masai and they remained your friends. But all I ever got from the Kisi was a spear thrust in the thigh, and it was the same leg that had taken a Boer bullet.

It was after that bloody slaughter of the elephants with the Wanderobo. I went north of the line and hunted in the Rift Valley. Up there I met a man called Carnegie, who had just given up his commission in the Gordon Highlanders, and who wanted to take up farming. I said I would find land for him if he would buy cattle from me once he was settled. And we drank to that and I went land hunting.

I found him some land, sold some ivory for cattle, sold the cattle to him, and was having another celebration drink with him when the DC from Kericho came in with an escort of police. He said that he had been attacked by the Kisi while collecting taxes. DC's men were always being attacked while collecting taxes, and this one was no happier than most were at the experience. I knew little about the Kisi then, and he was eager to tell me. He said they were bad-tempered and warlike, even raiding the Lumbwa sometimes, which shows what a high opinion they had of themselves. Their country lapped on the border, and among their spearmen were a few warriors armed with old, brass-bound muzzle-loaders they had taken from Arab slave traders decades before. The DC said sourly that he hoped the Government would make war on the Kisi once the Civil Servants found the money.

I asked him for permission to trade among the Kisi. He said no white man would last five minutes among them, but when he had gone, I told Carnegie that I would try anyway, and I left the next morning loaded with trade goods, escorted by twenty Lumbwa and accompanied by a boy who had been a slave of the Kisi and could speak their tongue.

The first of the Kisi villages was twenty miles from Carnegie's farm and we reached it about four in the afternoon. It looked formidable—round-top huts surrounded by a pointed stockade. The Kisi flooded out of it, waving spears and stomping, and when I had their attention for a moment I asked for wood and water. They were surprised, but no more surprised than I when they brought the wood and the water.

And they left us alone that night. I was giving myself a sponge bath in my tent next morning, gravely

watched by two Kisi children, when there was a great
thumping of drums and a gabble of voices from the
village. I toweled quickly and went outside. There was
a stocky, pock-marked villain with a great scar across
his forehead and two yellow hippo tusks hanging from
his temples. He said what did the Bwana want in his
country, and I said who was he?

He was En Dobee, Paramount Chief of the Kisi,
and still he wanted to know what I wanted. I said
that I wanted ivory and he thought about this and
finally decided that I could have my life, but he would
have my equipment and my carriers. The spears of his
warriors went up in approval.

I took a cartridge in one hand and a bead in the
other and I held them out to him. Which did he want,
a fight or a trade? He scratched his armpit and went
away and talked it over with his old men. Then he came
back and took the bead. I smiled and gave him a roll
of brass wire. He grinned, rattled the hippo tusks, and
gave me a fat bullock. He looked sly and then said that
I could do something that would make his people very
happy. The way he said it indicated that while he had
got a roll of brass wire, and I had got a fat bullock,
his people so far had nothing. Nothing had changed
their minds about me.

I asked him what would make them happy. He
said "Shoot some hippo."

The river was wide and milky with mud. I could
see no hippo, but I stood on the bank and trilled to
them and they came up one by one, two tons each
of rubber-wet skin and yawning jaws. I shot two bulls

and they went down quickly with the water red. It takes two hours for a dead hippo to float to the surface and while we waited I told my interpreter to inform the Kisi that when the bulls were dragged ashore my men would cut a little of the mutton-sweet meat for themselves. Then the Kisi could have the rest.

It was a wasted instruction. As soon as the hippo were ashore the Kisi fell on them like animals, hacking, slashing, turning their knives on each other until their blood was mixed with the hippos'. I knocked them down and swore at them, but it did not stop them, and I went up and found En Dobee and told him what I thought of the Kisi, which was very shortly put. He sent orders for the meat to be brought to me, and when it was stacked I told my men to take their share. Then En Dobee and his petty chiefs helped themselves, and the villagers fell on the rest.

Altogether I didn't think much of the Kisi, although I traded twenty small tusks from them. En Dobee's two sons came back with me to Carnegie's farm, and on the trek they told me about their people.

En Dobee had a brother called Majori. This Majori, it seemed, was the usual prince who was angry at not being crown prince, and he had quarreled with En Dobee. After some spear play between their followers they agreed to live apart. Not very far apart. Majori's nearest village was two miles from En Dobee's. The land between the two factions was barren and uncultivated. Nobody crossed it, no cattle were allowed to stray on it. The villages might have been two hundred miles apart.

If anything, Majori had the advantage over his brother for his village possessed a very powerful medicine man. The two boys told me that if I had the courage to visit Majori I would find four great tusks of ivory in his hut.

I told Carnegie that I liked the sound of those tusks, and he said that was fine, but if I were going back into Kisi country he would go hunting along the border of it in case I needed him.

I got some more trade goods and some cattle and went back. En Dobee was waiting for me with a big grin on his pocked cheeks. Also awaiting me was a message from Majori in the shape of a rhino club. The words that went with it said that if I cared to visit him, he would show me what a true Kisi did to a white man.

I sent back the messenger to say I would be happy to visit him, and En Dobee suggested that I take his sons with me. I trekked into Majori's country and the villages emptied behind me until there were hundreds of Kisi following along behind to see the play.

We camped outside Majori's kraal and waited for him. When he came out he was a fine-looking man in a yellow and blue blanket which he held like a toga. If he scowled at me he smiled at his nephews, and these made the air much more pleasant by explaining that I was not a tax collector but a hunter and trader. So I shot some hippo for Majori too, and there would have been no trouble but for his very powerful medicine man.

He came out of his hut and I was downwind of him and could smell him. Skulls hung from his waist, bones from his shoulders. His skinny arms and neck were decorated with the teeth of lion and leopard. He wore a kaross of monkey skin, and his eyes were yellow and his gums were white with saliva, and I knew from the look of him that he was going to use me as an experiment.

He stood there sneering and snorting, and the Kisi got behind him expectantly. He had his eyes fixed on my rifle, and I knew what was in his mind.

He turned and raised his skinny arms. He had medicine, powerful medicine, he said, to take away the tongue and the voice of my gun. He would make it as useless as a stick. And he turned to me and grinned, holding out his hand.

I put the .303 in it politely.

He thought the rifle was a muzzle-loader, and that all he had to do was blow the powder from the pan and replace it with dust.

He turned it upside down. He brought the breech close to his face and sniffed. He fingered the magazine. He looked down the barrel, and the cunning and the guile passed from his face, leaving an expression of venom that was oddly mixed with pathos. He raised the rifle above his head, swung with it, and gabbled to the Kisi, and then he handed it back to me, but with less arrogance and confidence than when he had taken it.

The Kisi looked on with interest.

I told my bearer to put an empty cigarette tin in the fork of a tree, eighty yards away. My first round knocked it from the fork, and a great grunt of surprise came from the Kisi. The medicine man shuffled his feet

and yipped once or twice. I had the tin put back, and
with the four soft-nosed left in the magazine I splashed
it on the tree trunk.

The medicine man began to scream, to jab his
finger at me, coming so close that his spittle struck
my face. I disliked him intensely, everything about him,
his pendant bones, his monkey-skin kaross, his tooth-
less mouth, and the smell of death's decay on him. I
had the happy wish to discredit him still further.

I went into my tent, took two water bottles, filled
one with water and the other with kerosene. I came out
and asked the doctor if he could make water burn. He
sneered all over his face. I allowed him, and Majori,
and a few other Kisi to drink from the bottle that
held water, and when I took it from him I switched it
with the bottle that held kerosene. I poured the oil
into a tin plate and set fire to it.

The medicine man started backing toward the village, killing me with his face, but I held his arm and
said there was one more thing I wished to show him,
and his respect for his reputation made him stay. I
painted his stomach with pure essence of mustard. As
soon as it began to burn he screamed and bounded
away.

Now all of this was out of a schoolboy's humor,
and is only made excusable by the fact that, had I not
proved myself to have stronger medicine than the witch
doctor, he could have easily persuaded the Kisi to add
my head to his cincture of skulls.

On the profit side I traded cattle for the four good
tusks that stood in Majori's hut.

We left in the morning, and the Kisi sped us with the beat of drums and the bray of horns. There was no sign of the witch doctor during this pleasant valediction, and as we marched I told my bearer to take a rifle and guard my back. We met the old man on the slope of a ravine, where a line of warriors stood at his back, prodding the air with their spears and calling loudly of their courage.

I stopped with my bearer, and I told the other boys to go on down the trail at the run. I called out and asked if these Kisi had forgotten my friendship with their chief. The witch doctor came down, hopping from stone to stone, skulls and teeth clattering. He came up to me and leaned on his ceremonial spear, and he looked sideways out of his dishonest face and said that he wished to be my friend. To prove this he was ready to give me a fat ox.

I stepped back from his breath, and as I moved he stabbed at me. The blade missed my stomach but went into my thigh, and the thrust was strong. I went back with it but I fired, and he skipped with a hop and a flap of his feet back to his warriors. I fired again, and my bearer fired too, and the Kisi dropped behind the stones.

The blood was coming out of my leg, but I felt no pain, only the sickness in stomach which you get at the sight of your own wound. I took a scarf from my neck and tied it above the wound, with a pebble on the artery. My bearer was pumping with the rifle, keeping the Kisi at their distance, and when their spears did some *thwanging* they fell short.

I got up, and we went down the hill to where my boys were waiting, and I fainted. I came to, very sick in the stomach, and I told them to pitch my tent and leave me, and go on to En Dobee for help. This, they said, they would not do. I told them that if they did not I would not hire them again, and that I would let it be known to Arab Changalla that I had no faith in them. They looked at me very sadly, and they pitched my tent and they went.

I lay there all night. I filled the magazine of my rifle and I put one round in the breech and disengaged the safety catch. I took more shells from my jacket pocket and laid them by my thigh, and I tried not to move much because I was afraid of fainting again. I watched the night through the tent flap and wished there were a fire.

Drums and horns sounded all night long, and I did not know why the Kisi did not come in.

En Dobee's men arrived at dawn, and carried me out on a blanket to Carnegie. He put me on the train and wired for a doctor to meet me at Lumbwa station.

I remember little of the journey. I remember my leg burning from groin to ankle. Then there would be no sensation in it at all, and I had the delirious notion that I had shed it, as a crab sheds a claw. Then it burned again, and it smelled. The doctor who met me at Lumbwa Station was full of whisky. He looked at the leg and he wanted to cut it off. He behaved as if all his life he had wanted to amputate a leg and had never had the opportunity until now. I told him that he was a drunken oaf, and that even if he were sober, and the best surgeon in Africa, I would not let him cut off my leg. All right, he said, I don't want the case. And he went away, probably to find more whisky.

There was a good Indian compounder attached to the African Rifles at Lumbwa, and someone brought him to me as I lay on the platform raving. By that time my leg was blown up with pus. I yelled and swore at him when he pushed in the drains and pulled them out, but he was a good and gentle man, and he saved my leg. When it was healed, it was bent like the branch of a mimosa tree, but Arab Changalla sent me some of his women and they massaged it day after day until I could straighten it and walk on it again.

❋ S E V E N ❋

Hit Him on the Knee,
If You Can

I could get two cows for a buffalo hide, said Jordan, and this is the hardest way of buying cows that I know.

The Lumbwa and the Nandi, the Kavirondo and the Masai, made good shields from buffalo hide, tough shields that could deflect a club or a glancing spear, and take the weight of a charging lion if the man behind had marrow in his bones. But the Lumbwa and the Kavirondo were reluctant to kill their own buffalo. An *elmoran* of the Masai would go out and kill a lion, but he preferred to buy his buffalo skin. Yet the Wanderobo, who would think many times before facing lion, joyfully slew the buffalo. There is no explaining this, except that fear is common to all men and they are incomplete without it, and the subject of their fear varies according to their imagination. But that explanation does no credit to the buffalo who, I truly believe, is more terrible than the lion.

However, the Bwana Mkuba killed buffalo for the Lumbwa, the Kavirondo and the Masai, and traded the

118

cows for ivory, and sometimes he thought it was a hard
way of getting ivory, and that his head needed exam-
ining.

The lion will not attack the buffalo, nor will the
leopard, that dog killer. The buffalo need only fear a
Wanderobo with poisoned arrow, or a white man with
a .500 Express, and sometimes a Lumbwa *elmoran* with
more courage than sense. But even these three may
change their minds after they have seen what a buffalo
can do to a man.

The buffalo is low-built and stocky, not more than
five feet at the shoulders and broad there like a wall,
with muscle not fat, and his body goes back in graceful
lines to the narrowness of his flanks. Black, he could
be no other color than black, a blackness that shines
and ripples as the muscles knot and move beneath the
hide. Seventeen hundred pounds of cunning and hate
and aggression, a body so powerfully built and compact
that even a .450 will not always pass through it.

His horns are the damnedest things. They spring
from huge corded bosses on his forehead, and make him
look as if he were wearing an old bush-hat pulled low,
and they sweep backward and swing upward to wicked
points above his flopping ears. The widest spread of
horns was got by Selous, I believe, and these measured
forty-one inches, over sixteen of them across the face
of the boss. Between the bosses there's not more than
half an inch free of horn, a narrow gateway to his brain,
and it is true that if you hit him there with a hard-nose
you would kill him, but who could hit a mark like that?
Hit him on the knee and that will stop his charge—if

you can hit him on the knee—and that is no easier than hitting him between the bosses. But to bring down a black buffalo bull is a great moment in the life of a hunter. Cut off his arrogant bushed tail and it will make you a thick soup richer than ox, richer even than giraffe tail.

The weight of his horns seems to pull down his head, yet see them go up when he gets your scent, and they lie back on his shoulders, his blunt muzzle points dripping with saliva, eyes bloodshot, red nostrils flared. He can swing those horns like sabers, and his heavy body is a feather when his narrow legs begin to move.

He has one emotion, hatred. He hates and he kills in his hatred, and he will track *you* to kill in his hatred. A devil with twenty-twenty vision, swimming a river like an otter, grazing in a glade with his dark red cows, hiding in a swamp watching you, waiting for you. Bounding like a frisky colt when the flies worry him, standing like a rock in the second before his charge.

And I got two humped-back, docile cows for his hide.

I say the Lumbwa preferred not to kill their own buffalo, but a man must sometimes challenge the thing he fears and I have seen an *elmoran* dueling with a buffalo bull, spear in one hand, sword in the other, lunging, stabbing, dancing, and killing sometimes, and sometimes being killed.

I said, "Who could hit a mark like that half-inch between the horns?" And, having said it, I must say that I have made such a shot, but not through skill, not through anything but chance, and had I not had that chance I would be dead, dead in a particularly foolish and unpleasant and horrible way.

I was following the blood-spoor of a wounded elephant, my head down on the trail, when I rounded a bush and faced a lone bull buffalo. The scent was away from him, and he only *saw* me, and not scenting me was puzzled by what he saw. He was old too, a lone bull, an outcast, and there were gray scars like weals on his body where he had fought for and lost his leadership.

I suppose we were six yards apart, and because the wind was toward me I could smell him, a strong and not unpleasant scent, the smell of the sun on his hide. I was the first to move, again perhaps because he could not scent me and did not understand. It was a snap shot, and I did not see the sights. I fired once and saw him go back and over, his narrow, pretty legs sticking up. My bearer ran up to him and put a finger in the bullet hole, between the horns, and cried *"Piga, Bwana!"* with great pride. But it was a fluke shot and I take no credit for it.

If you have an eye for the trail, for a pebble kicked from its dust bed, a broken blade of grass, clear spoor in the mud, warm droppings, faint channels where the earth is broken, if you can read this sort of thing, then there are books written on the face of Africa, and there are few more dramatic than that written by buffalo spoor.

See where trails cross. First a man's—feet slow-moving, the trace of a spear haft in the dust—and then a later track as the buffalo gets the scent of man and turns from his own trail to follow. You follow, with the buffalo spoor in pursuit of the man's until you meet the chapter end, the buffalo spoor hazed as the bull went into a charge, a scurry where his horns met the man, and there the bones scraped clean.

Or sometimes the man's trail ends at a tree which he had reached and climbed. The bark is stripped, the roots are dragged from the earth, weakened by the battering that has gone on until the bull has shaken the man from the branches and killed him.

He is cunning, the buffalo. He will tree a man thus, and charge, and bellow, and slash; and if the man does not fall, the bull will use guile. He will turn and trot into the grass as if the sport bored him, and he will wait there, hidden, until the foolish man climbs down.

But the natives know this trick, and once they are treed by a buffalo they lash themselves to the branches with their sword belts or their loincloths. They roast in the sun, their mouths crack with thirst, they lick their own sweat, the belt cuts into their flesh, and their voices, the voices which have been crying for help, dry up. And when the bull sees that his trick has failed he charges again and again at the tree, and so the game goes on, for twenty-four hours if necessary, until the buffalo plays his foulest card. He drops his excreta beneath the tree and waits for the maddened man to be driven down by the unspeakable odor of it.

I have been treed more than once, but armed with an Express rather than a spear, I have held the advantage, not the buffalo.

A picture showing John Alfred Jordan in the uniform of the Cape Mounted Police. The date was 1900.

Tent-mending in camp during safari.

Jordan mounted on a Somali pony.

These elephant tusks average eighty pounds apiece.

A pygmy standing between two bearers.

Only the Wanderobo had a contempt for the buffalo. When they killed him it was a beautifully staged gladiatorial contest, although something the Romans never saw in the Circus Maximus. The Wanderobo were brave, but when they killed the buffalo they used more wit than bravery, turning the animal's cunning and his hatred of man against him.

They hunted in parties, armed with bows and with the *semi*, that soft-iron sword which was like a Scots broadsword without the basket hilt. They would find a glade on the edge of the forest where the dried droppings and the flattened grass showed it to be a buffalo halt.

There one of the Wanderobo would strike his sword into the earth and hang over it his cape of monkey skins. Then he and his friends dropped back into the trees, their bows strung with heavy-headed, poisoned arrows. They would wait there silently for hours, and once when I waited with them, I felt my muscles harden and my bones lock, and I knew that if the buffalo came, and if the plan did not work and it found me, I would be able to do nothing to stop its charge.

That morning we waited for three hours, until I heard the grass whispering and saw the tops of it swaying. I saw the horns go up as the herd scented the man-smell on the swaying cape. It was a strong scent and they broke cover angrily. The black bulls came to the front, the red cows dropped back into the grass. The bulls snorted, lowering their great heads,

blowing at the dust, pawing. They saw the sword and
the skins and they charged. The leading bull caught
sword and cape with a right sweep and tossed them
into the air, and the bulls were within the circle of the
Wanderobo.

From behind every tree the bows were plucked,
and the arrows went into flank and belly and shoulder.
The vegetable poison was fresh; it had to be fresh or
it would be no more dangerous than treacle. Once I
shot a bull that had three arrowheads buried in the
muscle of its right shoulder, and there could be no
doubt of what it had done to the Wanderobo that
fired them.

But this morning the poison was fresh, and with
each volley of arrows the bulls threshed madly in the
glade, horning each other in their agony, and this
strange and terrible struggle, with its bellows of agony,
with the Wanderobo stepping from cover to fire at the
buffalo almost within range of the horns, this went on
until there were eight bulls down, throats stretched,
mouths open. And the others broke and ran.

An old bull once held me captive in a tree. I had
heard of its guile and cunning, and perhaps I allowed
it to tree me because I was young and I did not believe
there was an animal more cunning and resourceful than
man.

I was tracking elephant along the reeds of the
Taveta River in Ukamba. The reeds were yellow sword
blades and so thick that you could not see more than
a foot into them. My bearer suddenly shouted and ran

for the nearest tree, swinging into it. A fine black bull, with horns like the front of a locomotive, crashed out of cover with head down, charging for the tree. He hit it and it shuddered. My boy screamed and climbed higher.

The wind was in my favor, and the bull did not know I was there. I went down on my knee and fired as he charged again at the tree. It was a badly placed shot, and I saw the round go along the left shoulder, dropping a dark curtain of blood on his hide.

It annoyed him, and he brought his body round with flanks tense, his head up and nostrils wide. He swung his head from side to side, scenting for me. I crawled through the reeds to another tree and climbed it. My bearer cried out, *"Piga,* Bwana! Shoot!"

He had tied himself to the branch and he looked safe enough, although every time the buffalo charged the trunk, tree and bearer went oddly out of focus. I wanted to see if these stories were true. I was light-headed. I cheered and waved my rifle every time the bull charged. And it was true: he did everything the natives claimed. He charged, he slashed at the bark, he trotted away cunningly, he fouled the earth.

And then he scented me and punished me. He battered my tree and reached up and slashed at the bark, and my bearer looked across with relief and approval. Then the bull stood between us and I shot him. It was a good, clean shot, and he was ten yards away, legs straddled. It hit him above the shoulder, a downward shot that dropped him at once.

When a buffalo kills, he is not content with the act of killing. His hatred is insatiable. With his horns, his sharp hoofs, he strips the flesh from the bones, slashing, stamping, tossing.

This I know. When I was up by Thysville, on the highest point of the Congo Railway, about the time when I was determined to get that King Elephant, I saw enough to believe.

I was out one morning, and the day suddenly fell into one of those gentle, suspended moments of silence you get in Africa, tranquilizing the mind and immobilizing the body. I sat down to smoke, and then I saw the vultures dropping down to a clump of bush two hundred yards away. I heard the slow slap of their wings, the tearing of their beaks, and I got up with the peaceful mood gone out of me and nothing there now but disgust. I went over, and the vultures watched me, hopping back from the raw flesh, flapping up with hoarse *crawking*.

They had been eating a man, or what must once have been a man. The tracks said plainly how he had died. His old, brass-bound muzzle-loader was twisted in the dust, its stock splintered. He had wounded a buffalo, just wounded it, and the wiping rod in the muzzle showed that he had been trying to reload before the charge. But the buffalo had caught him, tossed him, and then held him on the ground with forehoofs while the horns ripped and slashed until the bones were white.

We found the buffalo a mile away, dead at last from the native's shot, if that was any comfort to the man's spirit. Seeing how he died, I doubt it.

The dirtiest fight I had with buffalo was along the
Amala River. I had some Lumbwa with me, and two
of them followed the honey bird into the forest shortly
after dawn. They found a hive and one went to gather
dry grass. He heard a yell from his friend and ran toward it. He found his friend on the ground, and on top
of him was an old black buffalo, plunging in a macabre
dance, horns sweeping, hooves stabbing. The Lumbwa,
the live Lumbwa, ran. He ran into camp shouting,
"*Soita*, Bwana! Buffalo!"

We went out, passing the dead warrior who had
been much liked, following the crashing trail of the bull
through the grass. Life is low-priced in Africa, but a
man is a coward until he avenges a friend, and my
elmorani stayed on the trail for two hours without
speaking until the spoor led to a swamp and a drinking
hole, and there it was crossed and recrossed by the
spoor of other buffalo.

My leading tracker was Arab Tumo, a Manga
Lumbwa of great courage and great renown. Mataia
had given him to me to be my tracker, and I was aware
that this was a great compliment for there was no other
elmoran among Mataia's people like Arab Tumo.

He was a dandy, but his vanity was the vanity you
find among good soldiers. On his forehead he wore a
flat, circular ornament of pelicoid shells. He kept his
buffalo shield well oiled, and its insignia bright. His
bead belt, with its two-edged sword, was cleaned daily,
and the sword burnished. His ankles and his armlets
and necklaces he polished with the leaves of *kiuvi*. He

had a way of twirling his long-bladed spear so that
it became a torch in the sunlight, and when he did this
he would sing of his victories. When he felt the day
deserved it—and these were days when his courage
had been tested—he would put on an ostrich face-
frame and white-beaded *mithanga* which were handsome ankle spats. And he would wear a horn snuff
bottle cleverly ornamented with copper rings. So you
will see that I have rightly called Arab Tumo a dandy.

Among his people he was known as The Slayer of
Rhino. He said he had killed sixty of these animals,
alone, and with spear thrusts. I believed him. I once
saw him at such a kill, when the giant swung out of
the grass at us and charged with pig eyes red. Arab
Tumo crouched before it, legs straddled, spear poised,
and as the rhino met him he sprang to one side and
drove that spear in behind the left shoulder, through
to the right hip. Then he stood back casually and
watched the rhino die.

I tell you these things about Arab Tumo because
you should know how fine a man was when you learn
of the bad thing that happened to him.

We waited at the drinking hole, crouching behind
a fringe of reeds, and Arab Tumo put out his hands
gently and parted them. I saw the muscles of his back
stiffen and his body become motionless, until the only
thing that moved were the flies on his shoulders. Then
he put up his hand.

I looked over his shoulder and I saw two mighty
bulls by the water hole. They had scented us, or they
had heard us, and they were suspicious, their heads

up, nostrils open, their horns brushing their shoulders.
Then, as my *elmorani* came up, the bulls saw the movement of the reeds and charged.

They came up from the water and I fired quickly,
with no exact aim, but hoping to halt them or at least
make them swerve.

One shot broke the foreleg of the leading bull, and
it went down with its right horn scoring the mud.
Before I could reload the other was among us, coming
in a little to the right of me. My gun empty, I went
face down in the mud.

I saw the body of Arab Tumo going up in the air
and over me, slowly, with legs and arms this way and
that, and the loincloth floating, coming down and falling
heavily in the swamp.

The buffalo was among my Lumbwa, and although
they were not men who chose to fight the buffalo, this
one they fought bravely. I heard it snorting. I heard
them shouting, and the *"Huw!"* as they drove in their
spears. I could see little in the reeds and the dust, but
the blackness of the bull, the sweep of horns, the glint
of spears.

I went down to Arab Tumo. His face was in the
mud and the mud was red. I turned him over and
wiped out his mouth, and my handkerchief was red.
There was mud and blood on him and I could not see
how badly he was hurt, but the blood came out of his
mouth.

Now there was no noise of the fight above us, but
one of the Lumbwa began to chant and I knew that
they had killed the second buffalo, and I called for them

to come down. Two came, and the others padded into the swamp to find the bull with the broken leg. We dragged Arab Tumo up the bank, and there was a gash on his thigh to the bone.

I reloaded my gun and as I did so the buffalo with the broken foreleg came out of the swamp. He staggered but the spirit was strong in him. He was going to kill someone, and as he lowered his head the only thing in sight he could kill was me.

I fired both barrels at him from five yards, and the recoil of the gun was terrible, something I had never known. It threw me on my back, and when I got up I was so surprised that I looked at the gun before I looked at the buffalo, who was down and dead anyway. One barrel of the Express was split, six inches from the muzzle where it had been choked with mud.

We had killed two bulls, but now nobody was happy. There was Arab Tumo with a gash on his thigh and blood coming from his mouth. Two more of the *elmorani* had been killed as they fought the first bull, ripped from groin to rib cage. And a third had his shoulder dislocated.

We buried the dead men, and we put a cairn over their graves, and we went back to camp. The guinea fowl I ate that evening was coarse in my mouth, and I could speak to no one. The Lumbwa sat about the fire in their blankets, and the blood still came out of Arab Tumo's mouth.

I have seen two buffalo fight for the leadership of the herd, and although it was a terrible sight, it was

clean and frank and there was no cunning in it, as if
they knew that leadership rested on strength and courage and power, and they fought to decide who had the
most of these virtues.

The fight had begun when I heard it and crept
up to watch it.

They stood with feet braced and horns locked,
and they wrestled so fiercely and so equally matched
that they were almost motionless, and the dust was
hardly disturbed by their hoofs. Their lungs pounded
like steam hammers. But one was much younger than
the other—as one is always much younger in these
combats, among men as well as among animals—and
slowly he began to drive the old bull backward. Slowly
at first, and then in short and swift rushes as he braced
his hind quarters and put all his weight and strength
into the push.

This the old bull could not take for long, and he
twisted and broke free, trying for an upward slash with
his horns, which the younger bull avoided. Then they
backed off, measured the distance and lowered their
heads. They charged at the same moment. Swing two
logs together, end to end, two huge logs, and you will
get the sound and impact of that charge. I have seen
this in other animals, in the elephant for example, and
I have wondered, and still wonder, how they withstand
the blow. I know the weight and thickness and the
strength of the boss that protects the forehead of a
buffalo, but why does its spine not buckle and break?

They charged and locked horns, and braced their
legs again in the dust, and their knees bent and their

heads went down. Their breathing blew the dust into their eyes.

Again they broke, and this time the old bull struck and ripped the other's shoulder, opening the black hide like butter. But he was young and strong and ambitious. They charged again, but this time I saw that the old bull was weakening. With every charge the shock threw him back, until finally he no longer met the charge and took it with his horns. He was caught broadside by the young bull and flung on his back, and there he lay with his tongue out.

The young bull did not kill him. To have thrown him and defeated him was enough. He lay there while the victor snorted, shook his head, frisked his rump, and trotted off to lead the herd, to breed from whatever cow he chose.

✳ E I G H T ✳

Four Miles of Darkness

I took the first film safari into Africa, said Jordan, the first real one, that is.

It was over forty years ago, and some moving pictures had been made there, and screened at the bioscopes, but they were tame, a few hundred feet shot by Norfolk-jacketed sportsmen. As I remember them they showed dogs chasing lions, or lions chasing dogs.

I was in New York arranging to trap some animals for the Ringling Brothers and for Barnum and Bailey, and I saw some films in the little Broadway theaters, and I thought that someone should put Africa on to that flickering screen, a film that showed Africa as it really was, and not as a coursing match between a lion and a dog.

I organized a party. It was not a large party. There was myself, a cameraman and his assistant. The cameraman was Pierre Sirois, a Frenchman, whom we called Pete. Tom Robinson was his assistant, and we bought a camera and a tripod and several thousand feet of film, and we set out for Africa.

As soon as we started upcountry from Mombasa I saw that the one real worry of this safari was going to be Pete. He knew all about filming, or said he did, and nothing about Africa. I knew all about Africa, or he thought I did, and nothing about films. The safari could have done with more balanced knowledge.

To Pete, very French and very European, Africa was a nightmare, a very hot and sunlit nightmare with appalling things coming at him out of the grass. He was very unhappy and it was no comfort to him to be told that he was a pioneer in his profession. There are people who just do not want to be pioneers.

His camera weighed fifty pounds, and had to be set up on the heavy tripod. Where it stood it had to stay. Yet all Pete had to do was to supervise this simple action and wait for animals. My problem was to get such animals past the camera slowly enough for Pete. He had a big Lumbwa *elmoran* as his bearer, a tripod bearer not a gunbearer, much to the Lumbwa's distaste. But this *elmoran* had been with me before and he chewed on his distaste.

We went up to the Lumbwa country on fast little Somali ponies, Pete bouncing unhappily, clutching his camera, his bearer trotting behind with the bright long legs of the tripod trailing. We decided to film elephants first; only they were large enough to satisfy our ambitions. And I thought we could do this with the least inconvenience either to the elephants or to Pete.

We went out at dawn with our porters and our spearmen, and we went through elephant grass higher than our heads. The ground was thick with vetch that snatched at our feet, and Pete looked up at the sky with the expression you might see on the face of a man who has suddenly fallen down a well. It was noon when we topped a hill and saw the herd below. They were going down to the swampland, a long, gray caravan, moving slowly, and there was fine ivory among them. I wanted to cheer. Pete looked at them. He got off his pony and lay down and put his hat over his face.

I said, "We'll go down to the swamp and find grass high enough to hide us, but low enough for the camera to clear." And this was a good idea, even Pete thought it was a good idea, particularly the part about the grass hiding us. So we went down, flanking the herd, and we set up the camera. The elephants came on and Pete looked at them through the camera and across the camera, and at last he began to crank the handle.

Perhaps I had overlooked many things, for this was the first safari of its kind, but this one thing I could not have overlooked for I knew nothing about it. As Pete cranked the handle there was a noise like a Gatling gun. It did not worry him for he was accustomed to it. The elephants, however, had never heard it before and a young bull shouldered his way to the edge of the herd, swung up his trunk and trumpeted. The other bulls took up the protest, and the cows added their treble notes, until the noise was like a gigantic but undisciplined brass band. The herd began to swing and sway irritably in the mud.

Pete stopped cranking, hand still on the handle, his face white.

Robby was just as frightened, but he decided that the thing to do in a case like this was shoot something. So he fired at a big bull, and a brave shot it was. It did not kill the bull, and the herd, which up to then had been looking for somewhere to escape this irritating clanking, went over to the offensive. They shuffled in an eddying circle, their trunks up, searching for us.

I shouted to the bearers, slapped Pete on the back to arouse him, and retreated up the rise. Pete's bearer loped along with the camera on his shoulder and a grin on his face. He put the camera down and pointed to it sarcastically. He said, *"Piga, Bwana!"*

The herd charged aimlessly over the spot we had left, and then split into small parties, circling, searching the air with their trunks, trying to catch our scent. Two stayed close to the bull that Robby had wounded, and it was these three who were determined to find us. They went about it patiently, circling in slow, shuffling movements, narrowing the circle until something stopped them forty yards from us. I wetted the wind. It was blowing our scent toward them.

Then up stood the brave Robby and gave them another shot with the .500. He brought down the bull he had wounded and it went over and shook the earth. The other two screamed. I was using a light 9 mm. which could not have stopped an elephant charge, so I aimed at the trunk of a cow that was standing unhappily in the dust by the fallen bull. Before I could fire, her little eyes saw the glint of Pete's camera, and she charged.

Pete said something short and breathless in French, and fainted.

The cow came in and picked up the tripod with such ease and grace that she reminded me of a lancer tent-pegging. She stood there swinging the tripod round her head, and beyond her I saw Pete's rump crawling into the grass.

Robby and I fired together and she went down like a noble ship. On her haunches first, and then on her forelegs, and you could see the strength slipping out of her. She trilled sadly, but the camera she kept aloft, until her head touched the ground and her trunk at last brought the tripod down gently.

We ran round her and picked Pete up, and we had to hold him up for his legs could not. It was three days before we could get him from his tent, and then he came out dapper in his bush-jacket, his polished boots and slanting topi, and he said, "How about filming something?"

I decided to go down to the Loita plains, where there were many gazelle and antelope and zebra in the yellow scrub, and there would be no charging elephants to worry Pete. We found giraffe on the edge of the plain, but they cantered away from the shining camera, with Pete shouting, "*'Old zem.'*" We followed them for two hours until, in disgust, I told Pete and his naked bearer to get into the bushes. Robby and I would go out on our ponies and drive the giraffe in. They would pass him, all he need do was crank.

He said, "*Vraiment?*" And I said, "Of course."

We circled the giraffe, coming in a wide sweep behind them and then driving hard, standing in our stirrups shouting. The giraffe went on smartly, with their stupid necks jugging. They not only stampeded past the brush where Pete was cranking, but through it, lurching away from him at the last second. We rode up through their dust and there was Bwana Mkuba Sirois with a wide grin. He said he had taken three hundred feet of film and had been too busy to be afraid. He explained that it was like that with a man. When he had something to do he had no time for fear. That was how it was, I agreed.

In that month the Loita plain was thick with game. You could stand on a rise and pick them out by the curl of horn or flash of rump fur. It was the scene that sportsmen dream about before they come to Africa and which, if they are very, very lucky, they do sometimes see. And I knew that all we need do was build a blind for the camera, in a thicket by a trail, and drive this game past Pete's camera.

I stayed with him and helped him set up the tripod. He fussed about it like a woman, crouching, bending, sighting. The beaters were out, and they scudded round several herds, bringing them gently together until the whole plain was moving toward us with the sun on flank and horn, and the air trembling. Even Pete was caught by the wonder of it. He stared at this river of animals and I knew that he had already filmed them, that he was now sitting in the theater with his legs crossed, and seeing this drive, filmed at great risk and great expense by Pierre Sirois. There was a faint smile on his lips. He was being modest about the applause.

I had my glasses on the herd. There were two, maybe three thousand animals out there, coming fast under a red dust cloud. They were coming straight for the blind, and they were not yet frightened. Then something alarmed them and they stampeded. I saw the stampede as a sudden lurch forward, so violent that it was as if they had been stationary until that moment. Now they were a torrent of red and white and black and gray and sweeping horns. Some were racing low on the ground, some bounding, and the beat of the zebra's hoofs, as they ran in a striped cloud on the flank of the stampede, was a rapid, desperate drumming.

I wondered why I could not hear the Gatling crank of the camera handle.

I saw why. Pete was determined to sell his life dearly. He had picked up a rifle.

I shouted, "For God's sake take the picture!"

He looked at me. He said, "*Comment?*" as if we had never met.

I shouted, "*Shoot!*" And since there could be some ambiguity about this I said, "The *camera!*"

He started cranking. He was lucky. He must have filmed several feet of the last gazelle as the herd swerved past us.

For a month Pete behaved nobly and nonchalantly. He filmed several hundred feet of placid impala, of hyena and vulture, of the camp and our boys, and I decided that perhaps he was now ready for something more exciting. We went to the Amala River to film hippo, but there was only an old bull in the water and he wouldn't come out. However, he blew water through his nostrils and flicked his ears at the flies, and these things Pete faithfully filmed, and I suppose that for an audience who had never seen a hippo blowing water and flicking his ears this could be very interesting.

We looked for buffalo, and I thought that here we would either have very good pictures or a very dead cameraman. It was hard to find buffalo. The land was lonely, rolling parkland as green as England except that the earth in the dongas was red. But the trees were spaced like orchards and the hills were barred with thickets as straight as hedgerows. Pete rode by my stirrup with his Lumbwa bearer trotting behind us, and Pete was very content. He talked of buffalo as if they were some sort of wild cow.

We rode thus until the bearer stopped and smiled. He had heard the honey bird, and he put down the tripod and went off into a thicket with his friend. They both came out quickly and behind, the thicket crackling, came twenty black buffalo.

Their horns were down and they were moody, but they were not going to charge.

Robby and the bearers went down in the grass. I got Pete off his pony and behind a tree. "Crank!" I said.

The buffalo were in a line along the grass, with an old black bull as their troop leader. The crank of the camera brought their heads up and they sniffed the air, they pawed the ground. The old bull saw Pete and began to kick the ground back. The noise of the camera puzzled him. I thought, if he charges the whole line will be up here like heavy cavalry.

So I fired, and the bullet struck back of the bull's shoulders and burned him along the spine. He snorted and led the herd at a gallop across our front. Pete filmed 250 feet of them before they had gone, and nothing had happened to convince him that the buffalo was not a cow, albeit *très formidable*.

I started after the wounded bull. I told Pete to stand his ground, he would be safe. I said that even if I did not bring down the bull in its charge and it reached them, then the *elmorani* would kill it with their spears. It was obvious that he was wondering what the fuss was about.

But I could not find the blood-spoor, and we mounted again. I got the Lumbwa out in a line, following the herd. They went forward with legs pumping, shields up, and now and then one of them paused to hold up a blade of grass, or a pebble, and shout that blood was on it.

Then my bearer called and pointed, and we saw a bull in the bushes. We rode at it, but he circled the bush, keeping his horns down toward us, and I saw the blood-line along his back. It was my wounded bull.

I told Pete to dismount and set up his camera, and then I rode at the bush and called my dogs up to drive the bull out. They went in yelping, but the bull came out before they reached the thicket, head down, bushed tail like a standard.

He went straight for Pete, and Pete's pony rose up, came down, turned and bolted. Pete decided to leave it, going round twice in the air before he touched the ground. The bull went at him, and I saw the turn of its head as it bowed for the toss. My bearer, who was carrying my .500, fired it into the bull's flank, and the buffalo turned and took the bearer on its horns. It threw him fifteen feet.

Pete screamed. On his hands and his knees he scrabbled toward a gully. The bull heard the scream, turned sweetly and came quickly at Pierre Sirois.

Now my dogs went for the bull! The Airedale snapped at the nose and the buffalo sabered it. The other three he played with, and they kept clear of him, snapping, and I knew another would be killed soon. But the buffalo saw my pony and put his head down again in a charge. I kicked the pony and led the bull away. I took it down the plain and across the stream into the forest, where I lost it.

I could not talk to Pete that night. My bearer had been a good man. Yet it was wrong to blame Pete.

Now Pete wanted lions.

I wanted lions too. What would a film of Africa be without lions? We heard them around us at night, but we never saw them. We met a Dutch hunter in the valley who said he had seen rhino in the bush, and he asked us what was in the shiny box. Pete explained the rudiments of cinematography, and the Dutchman smiled and said again that there were rhino in the bush. He said it with an air of *I would like to see more of this.*

We shot a big-horned rhino the next day before Pete had time to film anything, and we were following the blood-spoor when the Dutchman, who was up ahead with the tracker, shouted, and came back with the brim of his hat flapping. He said—and he breathed heavily saying it—that there was a troop of lions asleep on the other side of the grass.

But they were asleep no longer. The shout of the great Bwana Mkuba Dutchman had seen to that, and when we got through the grass they were standing up, swinging their tails and watching us without malice. Pete clattered with his camera and then pushed up his shoulders in disgust.

I said, "What's the matter?"

He said, "Too much shade."

I said, "Shall I ask the lions to move?"

He said, "Thank you, no. *We* are in too much shade."

We moved over to better light, but the lions grew tired of posing for their pictures and they yawned and went away into the brush. Since it was only a narrow patch I told the boys to beat it. I stationed six spearmen around Pete and we waited.

We heard the high shouts of the beaters, the clash of spear on shield. The noise came closer, and still with no sight of the lions, and I began to think that they had slipped away to the flanks. Then one of my spearmen raised his spear and beckoned to me. I went over. He did not move his head. He said softly, *"Simba!"*

Twenty-five feet away was a magnificent blackmane, half out of the brush, tail twitching. Nervous, but not too nervous, the muscles on his hind quarters were slack. I flipped my fingers at Pete, and he came up reluctantly. He pushed the toes of the tripod into the earth and sighted the camera on the lion.

The black-mane coughed, and behind him in the bush the others roared. It was a magnificent sound.

Pete cranked twice, and ran for a tree.

Black-mane saw the movement and turned. He was too big, too good to lose, and I stood up and dropped him pleasantly with a shot in the brain. The others roared back at the shot and then turned on the beaters. I saw the bushes swaying, and one by one the Lumbwa leaping up into the trees to let the lions pass beneath them.

That was the end of the lion hunt. It was also the end of the big film safari. Pete had run out of film. I asked him where it had all gone and he explained. We had films of natives, of the camp, of a hippo in a pool, of giraffe, yes we had fine films of giraffe, and there was the stampede, of course. I said, of course. At that we had more film than had ever been taken in Africa. Pete was going to be a great man. Pete was going to be a very great man once he got his film to Europe. It occurred to me that I might well be famous myself.

We went back to Nairobi and Pete found a dark room where he could process his films.

He was undoubtedly a good cameraman. I took his word for the fact that in a studio there was not his equal. But he had never filmed in the open before. He had taken thousands of feet of film with his camera set for indoor work under brilliant light.

Our elephant, buffalo, giraffe and gazelle were dim blotches on an almost opaque stretch of celluloid, four miles long.

✻ N I N E ✻

They Had Dug Two Graves

I've had to live with myself, said Jordan, and I've always wanted to be fit for myself to know. That's a quotation from somewhere, but it was tailored for what little philosophy I have, and I have tried to live by it. There is another quotation: that all things grow old but greed. If you read that in one way it may mean that the young are always greedy, and certainly I was young and I was greedy when I went hunting for gold. But I was greedy for life as much as the gold, and I had not yet learned to live with myself.

We had a hundred dollars between us, Jack Wrigglesworth and I, when we went gold hunting, and we had a camping outfit that a Boy Scout would sneer at. I was twenty-one or so, and that is a very good age to be, because you have the law to confirm what you have known since you were fifteen: that you are a man.

I have always found life a challenge, and I have accepted that challenge. Is there any other way to live? I followed a pattern cut by the men of my family. My grandfather took up land in Oregon when that beautiful land was young, and I have been in Oregon and hunted there. It is a good land, and I know that it gave my grandfather what Africa gave me. My mother's brothers were horse-ranchers in Montana, and another of my uncles went to Canada and had so much of the man in him that he drowned himself trying to swim his horse across a river in flood.

I went to school in Worcestershire. I ran away to sea three times. In the 'eighties boys were always running away to sea, and I had no more luck than the majority. The third time I did get taken on as a cabin boy to a three-master berthed at Bristol. But the boy who had run away with me wrote home to his aunt for money, and they came and found us, and my father got so damned angry with me that he made me walk all the way back to Bath. I was ten or eleven then, I suppose.

The last attempt I made to run away was successful. I was older and more resourceful, and I got to South Africa and enlisted as a constable in the Cape Mounted Police. Very fine I looked in breeches and strapped-up hat. I rode with Gorringe's Flying Column, and the Boers gave me a bullet in the leg to remember it by. I got my discharge and went fishing for Cape salmon with some Malays, and all the salmon we caught had to go in wages to the Malays.

I met Jack Wrigglesworth in Port Elizabeth. He reminded me of the heroes in the old Boy's Own Paper. He was handsome and clean and very English. He could be cold with a hard, aristocratic coldness, and then he would smile as he saw the ridiculous side of his own appearance. He was about my height, six feet two inches, and he could box just as well as I could, or at any rate neither could knock the other down. We were both very young, and our youth made us allies in a world which, we were sure, was run by and for the old.

An engineer from a Union Castle ship told us that there had been gold finds up in British and German East, and we listened and we counted our money. We bought a bell tent, some kit, two tickets on the *Printz Regent,* and were left with one hundred dollars between us. But that was enough for two boys who were going to find gold.

When we got to Mombasa they said, "What gold strike? You mean that dream a Hindu storekeeper had when business was slack?"

But we knew better. We slept in the bell tent. We spent most of our money on rail tickets to Port Florence. There we hired a canoe and paddled it two miles across the bight of Lake Victoria to Kisumu, and there we got a passage in a dhow to the German port of Shirati. I lost my heart to Africa, to the great green lake and the blue sky, the dark frame of the forest, the islands like jeweled studs, the night calls and the empty, resounding silences of the day. We passed an island where thirty thousand natives had died of sleeping sickness that year, and I knew that Africa had all the beauty and the brutality a boy's spirit could need.

It had gold too, and to find this we had first to see the Kommandant at Shirati. He was very *korrekt.* He issued us hunting licenses and prospecting licenses, and he was happy to inform us that one of his countrymen had already found gold and was now at Muanza, fitting out an expedition to search for the main reef.

We were in a great hurry. We hired guides and

porters and we made futile forced marches that blistered
our feet, and hid the blisters from each other. When we
got up among the Wachise, we were told that this German had gone through two days before. So we hurried
and we caught up with him, and he said he was not
looking for gold; he was a hunter.

He was hunting with very strange equipment, and
we smiled at him in our youthful cynicism, and we left
before dawn and pushed on, glad to be ahead of him.

Two days later we awoke to find that our porters
and our guides had deserted us. There was only Jim, a
Kikuyu who had come over the lake with us as our personal boy.

I think we were frightened, but we did not speak
of this to each other, and we went alone down the yellow plain to a Wachise village where an old chief was
holding council in his striped blanket. The color of it
took my breath in my throat; the sun on copper bands,
on spear points and ruddy plumes, on the blue smoke
and the purple bloom of the old chief's skin. He looked
at us gravely out of his wrinkled face and talked to us
as if we were as old and as wise as he. He scratched his
chest and advised us to go no further. He said that the
least we would suffer if we went on would be thirst.

We had never been thirsty, not the thirst when you
have no water and know there will be no water, and so
he did not alarm us. He shrugged his shoulders sadly
and said that he would give us porters, but we should
take much water.

The land was dry, dry, shifting earth and parched
grass clasped in clumps. The trees—what trees there

were—crouched on the earth as if they wished to shelter in their own shadows.

The water ran out. We traveled a day without water. We awoke the next morning to find the porters gone, and once more we were alone with Jim.

Now we understood thirst. Water became more important than gold. We could not have looked as hard and as desperately for gold as we looked for water. Yet it was gold we found.

Our tongues were swelling in our mouths, but we found quartz outcroppings with distinct gold traces.

And then we could not move. We lay in the tent and let the fever hit us, while Jim padded out to look for water. We were delirious that night, having swallowed enough quinine to kill us. We lived. But in the morning Jack was raving. I lay beside him, my eyes hardly able to see the cone of the tent, the flies coming in and crawling over the sweat on my face, and I listened to Jack raving. First he would laugh, and then he would cry, and then he would moan, and he went on talking, and crying, and laughing and moaning.

Toward noon the fever dropped in me, and I pushed myself up on my elbow and saw a line of trees on the horizon, a long, long way off, and I reasoned simply that where there were trees there must be water. I don't know how far away those trees were. Perhaps I never saw them at all, for if I saw them then why had we not seen them before. But I got up and I took a rifle and a water bottle, and I walked toward the trees that might not have been there.

I found trees. I found them so dry that the bark

turned to dust when I touched it, and they were dropping over a dry gully. The pebbles burned my hands when I fell on them. I prayed. I prayed aloud and I prayed for water. I offered nothing. I asked for water. I got up and walked along the donga.

I walked along the donga and I found water. A stagnant hole that the sun had sucked lower and lower until the sides were almost vertical, scraped by the hooves of zebra and gazelle. It stank but I drank from it, and I filled the bottle. The water gave me strength, and although I had prayed for it, I thanked no one when I found it.

The water refreshed my desire for gold. I found more quartz, a fine reef of it, and in the fever that was still in me I thought cunningly of the German, that hunter with the innocent face. I collected sticks and pegged claims for myself and Jack, and I made a drawing of the place in my notebook. And I lay down and slept.

It was night before I saw the tent fire again, and between us a fine gazelle, with head erect and elegant horns. I shot it, and the shot brought out Jim who carried it into camp.

Jack did not recognize me. I forced some water, some soup, and some more quinine into him, and he was calm and looked at me and spoke to me rationally. That is all I remember, his face looking at me and smiling, until I saw it again and it was no longer smiling. He told me that I had been raving for a day and a night since I brought in the water.

Thus it went on, a damnable seesaw. When I was conscious he raved. When I raved he was conscious, and neither could cheer the other with the thought of the gold up there in the reef by the water hole that was keeping us alive.

The old Wachise chief came at last. I saw him a long way off, two hours after I had awakened and found Jim gone and believed that Jack and I were now completely abandoned. But Jim had gone for the Wachise and the old chief's face was dark with shame because of the desertion of our porters. He brought us food and water, and Jack sat up and began to talk coherently, which means that we both talked about gold again.

We had both walked around death, and nodded to it, and yet we still talked of gold, and perhaps we were justified for a man should be rewarded for his suffering. We knew that we must get to Ikoma, the German post fifty miles away, and register our claims.

We were carried in two hammocks, but the fever came over us again on the evening of the first day, and when I came to, I heard German being spoken around me. I saw Jack stepping from his hammock and collapsing.

Then a day, maybe two more days out of my life, before I awoke to the sound of Jim crying. He was sitting on his heels beside me, crying, and touching me gently. I called to him, and he looked into my face and ran. He brought a German sergeant of askaris to me, and this sergeant said that Jack Wrigglesworth was dead.

I said, "You're a liar." I thought it was a trick to

rob us of the claim. I said, "You're a liar," and he shook his head. "Show me the grave," I said, "show me the grave," and they carried me in the hammock.

They had dug two graves, and mine was still empty beside Jack's.

I said they could have the gold if they found it. I did not want the gold or the country. In two days I asked for porters to carry me on an eight-day trek to Muanza. When the porters reached the town, they put me down by the roadside outside, and they went away to get drunk. Jim stayed, he stayed until at last he went into Muanza and bullied and threatened the porters so that they came back and carried me to the hospital. He was loyal, and his loyalty makes nonsense out of the fact that he later ran away with my equipment and most of my clothes.

Blackwater fever, said the doctor. He seemed surprised that I was still alive.

I remembered the gold when I was healthy. That is the way with gold. I registered the claims, and the filing was valid, but the Germans never recognized it. I came out of the hospital in rags, and no one knew where Jim had gone, except that he had run away with everything I had.

I was twenty-two, and Africa stretched to the north and the south and the east and the west of me. I was twenty-two and in rags, but I knew that I had found Africa and it had found me.

I went into the town and there a rolling, smiling, sweating Greek trader called Antonies—who should have been called Bacchus—bought me a bottle of champagne. We drank it and I knew that champagne is not for rich men. It should be drunk by young men of twenty-two who are broke and in rags. Antonies said, "Take what you want from the store and pay me when you can."

In the store was an Italian whose name I cannot remember. I know he worked for a skin company in Ikoma, which seems an oddly inconsequential thing to remember about the Samaritan who once lent me twenty pounds when I was broke.

❋ T E N ❋

Sixty Rupees a Day

You can ride a zebra like a horse, said Jordan, but something more than its stripes stops it from being a horse. It is a docile animal without guts. Yet it is beautiful sometimes, with its head up in the sun, its neck arched, and the short bow of its mane making it look like a war horse in a Greek frieze. It will not buck when you mount it, but what spirit it has seems to go out of it when it feels your weight. To halter it is easy. I would carry a short stick and push this into my zebra's jaws when I approached it, when the jaws opened to bite. It chewed on the stick and let me slip a halter over its head, and there was no more trouble from it.

There was a time when I trapped animals for circuses and for zoos. It was perhaps more profitable than ivory hunting, for you could get between two hundred and four hundred pounds for one zebra, and there was even more money in gorilla, lion and rhino. But it was a business—a business with offices, paper and letters—and the fun soon went out of it and there was nothing in it for me.

When I was in England one year I talked with Peter Chalmers Mitchell who was Secretary of the London Zoo at that time. We talked about a zoo without

154

*A river boat on the Congo River
at the turn of the century.*

*An old photograph of the
author sitting on a freshly
killed elephant.*

These tusks measured 11 ft. 6 inches. One weighed 154 lbs., the other 152.

An Arab trader, typical of the many who operated in Africa before 1900.

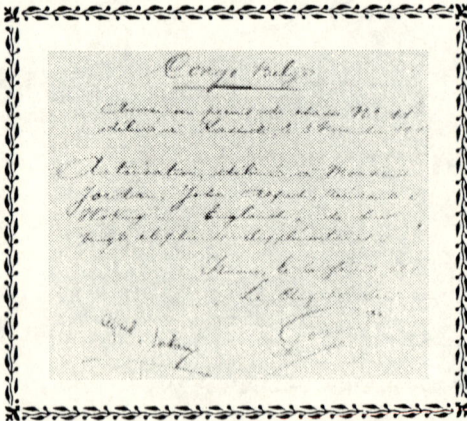

A supplementary license which permitted Jordan to shoot an additional 20 elephants. The license reads: "Authorisation is given to Mr. Jordan, John Alfred, a resident of Wokingham, England, to kill twenty additional elephants."

cages, a zoo where animals moved freely, and this was years before Whipsnade.

I had an animal farm in Africa, outside Nairobi, to which I brought the animals I trapped. I had giraffe, young rhino, eland, hartebeest, waterbuck, lesser kudu, duiker and Thompson impala. I had gazelle, leopard, hyena, jackal, cheetah, chimp, cat and mongoose. I had an ant bear which was the only one in captivity, a queer animal with a pig's snout and a lick-it-all-up tongue. My eland became so tame that I could brush and curry-comb them. I had a cheetah that followed me affection-ately, purring.

When I sent some animals off on the S.S. *Minne-tonka* for New York the freight charges alone were three thousand pounds, so you can see this was a very large business.

You cannot catch a full-grown rhino. If you did, it would kill itself in frenzied efforts to escape, or it would eat nothing and die to spite you. It is the same with gorilla, for these two animals have hearts that are easily broken.

I caught giraffe on the Loita plains by lassoing them, and the giraffe is an animal that can be beautiful only when it is stationary. The more it runs from you the more exasperated you become with its ridiculous shape. I caught hundreds of zebra in great drives. Some-times I had as many as three thousand Lumbwa tribes-men out on the plain rounding up zebra. We would build a kraal, a semicircular stockade with two wings leading to it, making a narrowing corridor. The wings were made of stakes planted twenty yards apart, and

the gaps between them filled with thorn. Then we left
the kraal alone for a week until the man-scent was gone.

When the day of the drive came, my Lumbwa beat
everything they found toward the stockade. Another
fifty boys hid behind the wings. On foot or on Somali
ponies the beaters stretched across the plain in a half-
moon five miles from horn to horn, driving in the animals, waving sticks with flags on them. It was a wonderful thing to watch them coming through the dust. Every
animal you can think of, driven along the corridor to the
stockade.

Then you cut out what you wanted and let the
others go.

It was exciting, and then I lost the taste for being
a businessman. I was happiest alone in the bush.

To watch the Lumbwa spearing rhino is to watch
an act that moves from dignity to comedy. The dignity
begins with the Lumbwa themselves, for they are a
handsome people when the sun shines on their skins,
on their black, white and brown shields, on their swords
and spears, on their proud faces and long necks. The
dignity, too, begins with the rhino, coming out of pre-
history, coming out of his tunnel of grass to die.

He is beaten out of the grass toward two lines of
elmorani who lean on their spears waiting for him, two
lines of ten men each, and when the noise of the beaters
gets closer, and the rhino is heard too, shunting in the
grass, then the lines of Lumbwa are no longer relaxed.
Each man is tense, and you know that he feels there is
no man left in the world to face this rhino but himself.

Out comes the rhino, pig-eyes red, feet pounding, head down and horn up, swinging a little to judge the thrust.

There are too many men for him, and before he can pick his target the first spear goes in. I have seen an *elmoran* step so close that the charging rhino brushes his loin cloth, and I have seen him drive in a spear far up the haft. Then the others come in, dancing, driving their spears, until the rhino halts with head swinging and horn driving but striking nothing. If he is lucky he may catch a warrior and put that long horn through the body, but he dies just the same, he dies and goes over with twenty spears in him like a pincushion, and the dignity is all gone and he is only comic in death.

The Maraquet country was never good country to walk through. Conge fiber grew to four or five feet, which is higher than the ridge of a rhino's spine, and the points of the fiber are like needles. I went into Conge fiber once with my boy, looking for guinea-fowl. I had a bottle of hock in my chop-box, and I wanted the sweet and tender flesh of the guinea for dinner. The fiber was full of them. They rose up, they drummed on the earth with their wings. We raised a cloud of them, and I got three with two barrels. But the shots roused a sleeping rhino and she blew through her nose and charged. She came out of the grass, her skin scarlet from the dried mud on it.

We forgot about the guinea and the fiber and went for a mimosa tree. The thorns stuck into my arms and neck, and I was slower than my boy who went through the thorns as if they were cotton wool and got to the top of the tree, jeering at the rhino. He stopped jeering when she hit the tree. Her horn went into it for six inches, and we felt her trying to lift it from the earth. She slashed and tore, and trotted away. She turned, shuffled, braced herself, and charged again.

She did this three or four times, and grew more angry with each charge. Then she trotted round and round the tree with her horn up like a halberd. Then she became bored and went back about ten yards to finish her sleep.

It was nine in the morning. I knew rhino. She could sleep there for six hours.

We tried shouting, but when we shouted the rhino lifted her head and snorted disagreeably. I said to the boy, go down and get the gun. He opened his eyes and shook his head. I said, "Five rupees," and he thought about this and went down the tree like a leopard. The rhino snored. The boy came back with the gun and evidently thought it was five rupees well earned. He handed it to me and went on up the tree until he was at the top again.

I had about a dozen Number Four cartridges in my bush jacket, and these were about as good against rhino as sprinkling pepper on her. But I thought that the report of the gun might at least scare her away, so I gave her one cartridge.

She came to her feet with a comic scramble, squealing. I gave her a second cartridge, but instead of trotting away she remembered us and the tree and she charged again. She hacked at the trunk as high as she could reach, and I leaned down, choking with the dust, and put two more cartridges into her face, hoping it would blind her.

It only made her more angry. The tree shuddered.

I remembered a trick I had once used with these Number Four cartridges. If you cut through them at the second wad, almost through them that is, the forepart is thus transformed into a solid lump which, at short range, can penetrate a two-inch plank.

I told the boy to come down. I swore at him, and he came down at last with the tree swaying as the squealing rhino hurled herself at it. I got the boy to lash me to the trunk so that my hands would be free. I made four cartridges and put two in the gun.

I leaned down through the thorns, and when she came up again, and stood there slashing and squealing, I thought of where to hit her. With a hard-nose, there are three places where you can be sure of killing a rhino, and only three: four inches back of the eye into the brainpan, into the spine between neck and shoulder, into the heart by the center of the body in line with the knee of the foreleg. I had no hard-nose, and I had no real choice of these shots. Her head was moving and this gave me no sure chance of the eye shot. She was below me, and I could not sight for the heart shot. But the aim between neck and shoulder was a good one.

I fired both barrels. She was thrown back with a terrible squeal, and the blood came out and washed the red mud from her neck. She thudded her head on the ground as if she were trying to shake something from the horn. She backed, dragged her head. I gave her the

remaining two shots, but the range was now too far, and
I don't think they did her any more harm.

Yet she had had enough, and she staggered into the
grass. We waited for half an hour, and then we climbed
down and picked up the guineas.

Crocodile was the only animal in Africa that made
me want to kill, and this was an impulse peculiarly
profitless. There is nothing about the animal that I admire, where there is always something about other animals. Even killing crocodile is a sickening business and
goes on too long before you are satiated.

They are foul and tongueless, with stones in their
stomachs to digest their food. They drag their prey
down and keep it on mud shelves below the water line
until it is decomposed enough for their tastes. There is
nothing about them to admire except their skin, and the
touch of that can put bad memories in my mind. It is
hard to know what frightens you about them. It is not
only their jaws; it is perhaps the knowledge that death
from them comes down under water in a green, choking
darkness.

I had come over Victoria from British East, and I
was in a bad way from malaria. I had some Masai boys
with me at that time, a Praetorian Guard of aristocrats,
and they looked after me as if I were a baby. When I
walked, as I did to walk the fever out of me in a mood of
black obstinacy, I held myself erect with two lion spears.
But the Masai smiled gently and took me to a Wa-Kia
village where I lay in a hut in a storm and thought I

would die. The Wa-Kia brought me eggs, and milk, and roast fowl, and I slowly recovered.

As I improved I sat on the shore and watched the crocodile, ugly snouts going through the water at six knots, and one morning when I was sitting on the bank improving my revolver shooting by firing at the yellow eyes, a canoe came in, a Kavirondo dugout with broad paddles flashing. The Kavirondo had seen this casual shooting, and they came ashore to say that Ol Dutchie, the Germans, were paying three rupees a head for all crocodile killed. This, the Kavirondo made plain, was not gratuitous information, and I rewarded them. They were worried too; the crocodiles were whittling down the child population of their village.

I worked it out. I should average sixty rupees a day. I thanked the Kavirondo and they paddled away.

I went over to Shirati, and I went too soon, for the fever came on again. In the bar someone said that there were two Frenchmen in the country who had started a hog ranch and a bacon factory from the profits of their crocodile shooting. I decided to ask the advice of these experts, so I took forty grains of quinine to steady me and went over. They had a large ranch and a good cellar. I admired the one and enjoyed the hospitality of the second. They said they had been miners in Madagascar but had come up to East Africa on the scent of rumors of a big gold find, the same rumors that had killed Jack Wrigglesworth. They had taken to shooting crocodile to pay their debts, and made themselves a profit of five hundred pounds.

They said I could have a canoe in the morning, and we drank hell to the crocodile.

For half a rupee a day each, I hired four Wa-Kia, German Kavirondo. Here were *black* men, not the chocolate of my Masai and Lumbwa. They were all above six feet and muscled like athletes, with fat, amiable faces and slyly humorous eyes. They were naked but for the brass and iron rings on their legs and arms, and tufts of cow hair like comic tails on their rumps. But they were superb boatmen.

When I said good-bye, the Frenchmen said, "We'll come along too. The crocodile got one of our boys this morning and we want to raise two hundred rupees for his widow."

They went on ahead in a ten-man canoe, and I heard them banging away up the lake. We went slowly along the bank, through patches of reeds, lotus pads and clear shallows where the fish darted in black fragments on the yellow bed. Tiny, lemon-colored birds spun from the lotus pads, and we started lavender-tinted crane. It was almost too idyllic for shooting crocodile. Then the insects came out of the reeds in columns, like smoke from a wind-bent fire, and we paddled offshore.

There was a mud island athwart the canoe's course, a flat with the water swirling about it, the dirty reeds like yellow stakes, and broken where the crocodile had made their slides. The crocodile lay on this flat like boats drawn up, their snouts down toward the water, some of them with jaws open in an immobilized yawn, and the parasite birds picking away at their teeth. There were dirty green ridges of hard hide running along the top of their flattened bellies, and their open mouths were rose-pink and dirty white. You could taste the stench of them.

I gave the largest a shot down the throat. He was perhaps sixteen feet in length, and death took him abruptly in a jerk that passed from the snap of his closing jaws to the last mighty swat of his tail. But with my shot the others went down quickly to the water, down through the glue of mud, quickly, like the launching of an armada of canoes, and they sank into the water and were gone. My Kavirondo applauded the shot politely, but I sensed they felt I had done something wrong. With all the crocodile gone from the flat this was no way to earn sixty rupees a day. You shot one crocodile, the others disappeared. There was no point in shooting them in water, you had to kill them on land where you could cut off their heads.

I learned what I thought was my first lesson in crocodile hunting. One island, one crocodile, and I hoped the islands held out. I got ten that morning, and in the afternoon I went ashore and walked up to see the Frenchmen. They had nearly thirty. The heads were in a bloody pile by the water. I said, "What's wrong with my shooting?"

I learned my second lesson. You take a large island, an island where the crocodile crawl up on the mud and push each other inland, and lie there blinking their yellow eyes, with their claw feet splayed, enjoying each other's halitosis. You shoot those closest to the water, and shoot others as they come waddling down. That way you can shoot many more than one on each island.

I shot eighteen before ten o'clock the next morning, and the heads filled the middle of the canoe and the blood slopped about our feet. We pulled inshore and I sent my boy and a canoeman across to the German post for the money.

I had heard the Frenchmen shooting across the lake in the haze, and I waited for them to join me at lunch. But while I waited, a hurricane came out of a black bar of cloud and whipped up the lake into cream, and the Frenchmen did not come. In the afternoon their boy came in and said that the Frenchmen had been drowned in the hurricane. I ran over to the Wa-Kia village where there was a half-drowned paddler from the Frenchmen's crew. His eyes were white with fright.

He said that the Bwanas had killed thirty crocodile before the hurricane hit, and when this happened they could not make the shore, so they shouted to the boys to return to the island they had just left. The wind was taking the water over and into the canoe and filling it. They flung out the heads and began to bale, but it is not easy to bale a dugout that is filling with water in a hurricane. It capsized. One of the Frenchmen and some of the paddlers went down at once, but the rest clung to the canoe.

I said, "What about the other Bwana?"

The boy said, "Gone."

He said the crocodile came up, hundreds of them, and one by one they plucked the men off that tossing dugout. The boy heard them go, and as they went they screamed, "*Mamba na kamata mimi!* Crocodile take me!"

Then there was only the boy and the Frenchmen left and they swam for the island. The boy reached it and lay on his face in the mud until he heard the Frenchman shouting. He looked up and saw the Bwana standing in the shallows, standing on one leg for the other had gone bloodily, and then he fell and the crocodile took him in a creamy pink swirl of water.

We sent out search parties. We found the canoe floating upside down, but we found no bodies. Why should we? They were lying on shelves below the water where the crocodile had frugally placed them.

I had liked the Frenchmen. They were jolly and they had made me welcome, and I had to leave the place where they had died. Africa is large enough to leave the places where bad things happen. I went down to Na Banji on a bight of the lake about twenty miles away where the Kavirondo said there were hundreds of crocodile, and I felt that there was now a personal issue between the crocodile and me.

I went down by Arab dhow, before a fair wind that sang in its terra-cotta sail. The natives came out of the village with drums beating and horns blowing to greet the Bwana Mkuba who had come to slay the crocodile. They feasted me on sheep and fowl and milk, and brought calabashes of eggs, and yellow bananas lying on green leaves.

There were screams in the night, and the villagers ran out with torches and clustered at the water's edge. There was a woman howling, tearing her breasts with her nails. The mud was gouged in a gully where her child had been taken by a crocodile.

The water was full of crocodile that morning, and before the sun set I had killed thirty-eight of them, and their heads, with slack jaws and lidded eyes, lay in a pile on the mud with the blood running back to the water. I killed ninety-five in three days, and on the fourth day there was no sign of them. For four more days there was still no sign of crocodile, and the natives held a great feast, and went down to bathe the next morning.

So they bathed until the crocodile came back at the week's end and took another child, and a cow. A native pulled at my tent flap soon after moonrise and asked me to come. I saw this Kiplingesque tug-of-war at the water's edge. The cow had gone down to drink and a crocodile had seized its nose. The cow had dragged the crocodile half out of the water and there they both stayed, the cow with legs braced, the crocodile with jaws clamped, tail threshing.

I shot the crocodile and the cow survived, though it did not grow a trunk.

And I shot more crocodile in the following days until the lust went out of me. My cartridges had gone and I was coming inshore with my last canoeload of heads, when a hippo and her calf came pinkly out of the water ahead and snorted at us. Evidently teaching her calf that this was how to behave when boats were around she blew water and made for us. The boys became hysterical, and went into an unhappy discord of paddling that filled the dugout with water. The bows went down and I shouted to them to swim.

I had been in the water a minute when I saw the

crocodile sliding happily off an island two hundred yards away. The strength went out of me and I began to sink. I went down, and I came up, and when I came up I shouted, "Oh, God save me!" This I cried several times, until I began to swim. I reached the bank, but I had lost my taste for crocodile shooting.

You can live twenty-five years in Africa and never be bitten by a snake, or you can die from snake poison within a week of landing at Kilindi. Or you can be bitten and still live twenty-five years in Africa, and this happened to me. Snakes are some of the most beautiful and terrible things in Africa, coils of yellow and emerald and black and scarlet. In their flat heads is indifference and malevolence in one paradox. If anything disgusted me about pythons, it was the slow enormity of them. They hung, draped idly on branches with heads poised, or lay bloated in the grass for their long sleep.

I blew one off the roof of my hut once, with the first barrel of my Express. It slithered down and coiled itself and uncoiled itself, with jaws open in milky saliva, until I shot it again. The coils wreathed like springs even while my boys skinned it. I have seen a python on her off-white, leathery, oblong eggs, her head coming straight out of a pile of motor tires, and her eyes with a furious glaze on them.

The mamba that bit me was a small thing, two feet long and shining, like a heavy hide whip, but green, a beautiful green like the rich undergrowth of the Ituri forest. It had a flat head and a pretty scarlet tongue.

I had been trading on the borders of Uganda, trad-

ing and recruiting Kavirondo workers for a blasting
contract I had obtained from the Uganda Railway. I
had a thousand Kavirondo enlisted, and a caravan of
hides and skins, and I was feeling very good, which is
always the moment when you should take care.

I had dined one evening with the French Fathers
and came back to my hut full of their good wine and
their good talk, too excited with the success of things
to sleep. I lay under my netting smoking until midnight,
and then I climbed out to write some letters. I climbed
out in my bare feet, which I should not have done. I
wrote for an hour or more, and then I called "Boy, *lete
chi.*"

He brought the tea and put it on the table, and he
looked down at the floor and said, "*Njoka*, Bwana!"

If he had said it softly, I would not have moved,
but he was frightened and he shouted it. "Snake, Mas-
ter!" and I moved my feet instinctively.

I moved and I looked down and I saw the green
whip snap of the mamba. It bit me, a small bite on the
small toe, and having done this it slid casually toward
the door. I killed it with a club.

My boy stood in the middle of the room staring at
me. I thought: The damned fool thinks I am going to
die; he is standing there waiting for me to die. And I
thought: I *am* going to die, that was a mamba.

I knew that the nearest doctor was forty-five miles
away, and that by the time he could be called and come
to me, I would need one of the French Fathers to say a
nunc dimittis over my thorn grave. So I took my skinning knife and I put my foot across my knee, and there

were the fang marks in the toe, faintly pink, and no pain yet except a nausea in my stomach that was largely fear.

I cut out the fang marks. I cut down to the bone, and I shouted to the boy to bring me a stick from the fire.

He brought it, blowing on it. He was blowing on it because he knew why I wanted it, and I took it from him and I pressed it on the cut. I swore and found great relief in swearing.

I stood up and padded about the room. I said, "Keep calm, Jordan," and I poured myself a brandy. Then I lay on my bed under the netting and stared at the ceiling, and told myself, "This will be no good. You've just done what you've read, what others have told you, but it is no good; it never was any good. They all died in the end, all those knife cutters and cauterizers." I tried to think of the men who, I knew, had survived a mamba bite, but I could not remember their names or their faces.

I lay on the bed until dawn. I remember that I saw dawn through the door. For a second, a very long second to a man who believed he was dying, it lay like a bolt of crimson cloth at the foot of a gray sky, and then the light went on all over the world, and the sunlight came yellow and green and brown, and I rolled over to be sick. My foot and leg were swollen to the knee, puffed until the skin was waxen tight, and I burned. I was sick again, and then again, and I said, "You'll die all right, Jordan, if you lie here."

So I stood up and *walked* on that damned leg. I

walked on it as if I hated it, which I did. I told the boys I was going to walk to the doctor, and they fell in behind me as if this were some strange death ritual that all white men followed. I was a brave man. I walked no more than two yards, and then I got the boys to sling a hammock on a pole and carry me. We had traveled ten of the forty-five miles when we met Henderson, the doctor, coming toward us. That is the luck I had in Africa. He was on his way to Mumia to treat an Army officer for blackwater.

He looked at my foot and seemed happy about it, happy the way doctors are when they don't want you to know what they are thinking. He said that the knifing and the cauterizing had been wise, and he gave me something, or I believe he did; I was past knowing. But I heard him telling the boys to hurry on to Port Florence.

I think the officer died of the blackwater before Henderson reached him.

It was four days before my boys carried me in to Port Florence, and with every dawn there were less carriers than there had been at dusk. They had worked out the logic of the journey, and their conclusion was irrefutable. The Bwana would be dead before Port Florence was reached—why carry him? The last one deserted in a village outside the Port, and the headman sat by my hammock for a long time before he sent in word that I was there and that I was dying.

But I was not dying; the poison had gone, and I was suffering from fever, from a cut and burned toe only. This was nothing; it would have healed in a week in England, but nothing heals quickly in Africa where sickness breeds on open flesh, and for two months that wound opened and closed until it finally allowed me to live and walk again.

So I went back to blasting rock. It cost me fifteen hundred rupees to register my Kavirondo, and another fifteen hundred rupees to equip them with water bottles and blankets. The first rockfall I blasted nearly took a freight train from the rails below, and I had an interesting discussion on blasting and railways with the engine driver, who had conclusive evidence to support his point of view. His engine was standing on its nose.

Then the rock was like iron, and the Kavirondo became bored. They were bored, and they ran away when the Nandi war parties came pounding through the forest. The Nandi raided my camp at night, and I had to crawl on my belly and empty my shotgun into the bush at them before they let us alone.

That was not all. One of my workmen sat brooding on his troubles for a whole day, and at nightfall he decided that the best way out of them was to kill me. He stood up and generously informed me that this he would do. He was six feet six inches, and I suggested that the headman tie him up. So he was tied up, but he broke the thongs and came leaping across the fire at me. I hit him with a crowbar.

Nothing went right after that mamba bite. I asked myself what I was doing blasting rock for a railway. Why wasn't I hunting? So I sold the contract and was glad to be rid of it.

The turn of the century brought railways and steamships and telegraphy to East Africa. It brought sportsmen, like Teddy Roosevelt, who cut another notch on the stock of his 9 mm. Mauser every time he shot something. Those years filled the gun rooms of Britain and America with the head and horns of eland, gazelle, kudu, impala and rhino. They brought the hunt for the rare, and nothing was more rare than the bongo, a beautiful animal, deserving of a less comical name.

I had come in from the Ravine and I heard that Rothschild, who collected his trophies from a distance, wanted a bongo skin. His agents at Mombasa were ready to pay a high price. The first thing, however, was for me to discover what the animal was. Someone gave me its Latin name: *boccerus Eurycerus,* which was intriguing but not informative. Someone else said it was the largest of West African bushbucks.

Then the Wanderobo said they knew this animal. To them it was sometimes bongo, a corruption of Swahili for bushbuck, but more often *signoita.*

And Bwana Jordan went hunting bongo.

No one had shot one before, no one had a whole skin. A DC had bought a piece of hide from the Wanderobo and sent it to the British Museum, but there was a faint fame waiting for the first white hunter to bring down a bongo.

It is as unlike a bushbuck as you could imagine. A first-class bushbuck has horns of perhaps fifteen inches. Signoita horn will go to thirty-five in the male and twenty-five in the female, and they are magnificent horns, curved and as white as ivory at the tip. The skin is chestnut, a chestnut fresh out of its green envelope, and with the same sheen on it. Chest, muzzle, and legs are white-marked, and below the douce gentle eyes of the beast are more pretty white markings. It is a beautiful thing, with grace, delicacy and courage, and it is never seen outside the deep forest, never seen afoot except at night or at dawn or at dusk.

Rothschild promised to be very generous to the hunter who brought in the skin of such an animal.

I went up to the Mau Forest and found some Wanderobo, and we talked about old hunts. We talked about elephants, and famine, and finally we talked about the bongo. The chief said his son, Wiana, would take me to the animal, but it would cost me a milk cow.

Wiana armed himself with a five-foot bow, a broadleaf pouch for honey, a quiver of arrows, a burnished *semi* and a happy smile. We took four dogs with us, loping, rag-coated, yellow animals with up-pointed ears. Nothing can beat these dogs on a single scent, and nothing can keep up with them when they raise it. The Wanderobo hang bells from their necks and follow this pleasant music to the kill. The bell never alarms game. Forest animals are nervous, but they are also curious, and they will wait to discover the origin of an unfamiliar sound before running from it.

We trekked hard through the forest. We found clean, neat tracks of the bongo, but never saw him. At dusk on the third day we shot a hartebeest and Wiana skinned it and cut out the liver. He roasted it on a stick and we ate it together. We put the rest of the carcass in a tree, and we built a huge fire and lay with our feet to

it, on soft leaves and fern, and in that night with the
forest around us, and the fire climbing high and yellow,
I was as close to Wiana as I have ever been to a man,
although we said little to each other.

At six in the morning we followed the spoor, and
Wiana went out with the dogs on a beat. I heard the
yelp of them and the tinkle of bells, and before I was
ready for him the bongo came out of the trees like a
fine chestnut horse on slender legs. It was too easy. I
sighted along the Mannlicher and brought him down
with one shot in the head.

He was nine feet six inches from nose tip to tail.
His horns were twenty-nine and one-half inches. There
was no flaw in his hide, the white markings were like
lamb's wool, and the chestnut redder than any red you
could find on the best impala.

I counted the nine white stripes over his back and
sides and quarters, and I strutted. There was no one to
strut before, but I strutted. I was the first white hunter
to kill and bring in the skin of this animal and I had the
right to strut.

Wiana grinned, and beat the dogs away, and got on
with his skinning. I grinned and could not smoke my
pipe for grinning. I had brought this bongo down with
one good shot, a good clean shot, the best I had ever
fired.

We put the head in a tree, and Wiana rolled up the
skin. It weighed fifty pounds.

I told Wiana to bring head and skin into the post
the next day, and I went on to brag. A bodyguard of
Wanderobo brought in this trophy. The Earl of War-

wick was at the post with a safari, and there was much posing for photographs, with Bwana Jordan standing by the head and skin of his bongo. And would I please sell it to the Earl of Warwick? Not I. I was getting a cable off to Rothschild in Paris.

One thing had I forgotten. The bongo, that chestnut beauty, was not mentioned on any game license, and no man had the right to shoot him, which was something the bongo did not know. When I got to the Eldama Ravine Boma, my skin and head were officially seized on the orders of the Provincial Commissioner, and I went away in disgust and anger.

Weeks later I heard that a skin and a head had been sold for fifty pounds at public auction, and later resold for two hundred and fifty. I had heard of no one else shooting a bongo, but there they were, auctioning a skin.

The Trouble Was, Men

There was a big fellow called Hoonan, said Jordan. He had been in the Irish Fusiliers, and perhaps I should have killed him when he gave me the chance, if you think it is charitable to save a man from suicide in this fashion.

That was the trouble with Africa then, men—men like Hoonan.

It was after the Government of British East had finally done something about the Kisi, conducting a desultory punitive campaign that was a dirty business of heat and fever and burning huts. I was in charge of some Masai and Lumbwa levies, and I was glad when the campaign was over. It only lasted a month, and the Masai and Lumbwa went back to their villages with the cattle they had earned, and I had a longing to go over into German East and find ivory.

I took a man called Saunders with me. He was young and he was a drunkard, but he had that wistful charm you find in some wastrels, and I liked him. He drank and he stole. He stole once too often in Nairobi and the citizens decided to reform him with tar and feathers, but I talked them out of it and took Saunders across the lake with me.

176

We went on the *Winifred,* a pleasant, white-waisted steamer which puffed around the lake like a visiting dowager, paying calls on Kampala and Entebbe and Shirati and Muanza.

We got off at Muanza, and it was beginning to look like a cross between an Arab bazaar and a Bavarian village, with shops and beer gardens, a market with carmine mountains of peppers and yellow ranges of rice. The Customs officers welcomed us by taking away our rifles, and there was a great deal of heel-clicking and back-straightening, and orders to come down and have the guns registered in the morning.

I went up into the town to find Monsuri. He was an amiable Dervish Arab, who had been an officer in one of the German native regiments when he was younger, and I had met him and drunk with him, and traded ivory and rhino horn to him years before. Now he was fat and complacent, and the resident of a fine brick house that contained a latticed zenana for his hundred wives. He had thirty trading stores upcountry under Greek managers, and in his bomas there must have been thirty thousand cattle which he had bought from the tribes at three rupees a head.

A dollar was the poll tax which the Germans put on native cattle. To pay it the tribes sold the cattle, which may not be logical economics, but it at least kept them from a three-months' sentence of hard labor on the roads, this being the Germans' method of tax enforcement. Looked at in this way you might say that Monsuri was a philanthropist.

I brought him a musical box, and although I real-

ized that it was a poor gift in face of his new wealth, it
delighted him. He played it all the time I was there,
cuddling it on his lap below his fat belly. I had also
brought him some gold, for he collected English sovereigns as a hobby, but I was not able to give them to him.
They were not in my pocket when I went for them. My
boy worked his toe into the ground and said that he
had seen Bwana Saunders feeling in the pocket.

I found Saunders drinking beer in the town, and
Hoonan was with him. Hoonan had a bad reputation. In
British East it was said that the Germans paid Hoonan
to give them information on affairs in British territory,
and this was probably true. He was a big, red-haired
man with the body of an ox, and an oddly articulated
way of moving his limbs that showed the punishment
he gave his body with drink. I ignored him and I asked
Saunders for the sovereigns.

Hoonan got out of the chair and it went back on
the floor behind him. What did I mean by calling his
friend a thief? Was I after a fight? He thought the questions would be better understood if he took me by the
throat. I hit him very hard at the side of the neck and
he sat down among four German officers who were
drinking tall-glassed lager. Hoonan lay there with the
beer running on him.

I walked out of the bar, and Hoonan got up from
the floor and came after me. He was a big man but he
was drunk, and he came at me too quickly, so that I
bent down and helped him over my shoulder with a leg
throw. He lay there breathing heavily. The Germans
came out too, and one of them, who was very pink and

well scrubbed, and had short gold hair on the back of his neck, suggested that I fight a duel with him.

I went back and told Monsuri, and he smiled and he said he would settle this small matter about the duel. He had friends. I hoped he had good friends for my reputation was low enough in German East. The Germans had a good colony there with docile natives, but I did not like the way they had done it, and if they did not suspect me of ivory poaching they would still have resented my opinion of their methods. I knew one of their commissioners upcountry who formed a native band, a big brass band with tubas and euphoniums, and uniforms that would have done credit to Potsdam. Every evening the band paraded before the Commissioner's veranda, and waited for him to come out with a case of beer and a Luger. One shot from the Luger was the signal for the band to play. It played sentimental German *lieder,* and student songs, and military marches, and its orders were to go on playing until the Commissioner fired another shot. But he never fired the shot, he got drunk, and the band played until one by one the musicians fell exhausted. Every evening Ol Dutchie's hand was heavy on the African.

That was why I worried about the well-scrubbed young officer who wanted to duel with me. He meant it.

Yet Monsuri settled it. Most of the Germans owed him money, and even a German will not offend his creditors. Monsuri told me that the young officer had been told to forget the matter.

Hoonan woke me up in the morning. He came in

with a revolver which he waved at me, and he dealt a
little too long on the pleasure it was going to give him
to shoot me. His face was raw from the fall he had taken
on the flint path, and where the flesh was not red and
bloody it was yellow. Dawn, however, is not the time to
tell a man that you are going to kill him; he is not likely
to believe you, and since I could not believe Hoonan I
got out of bed, reaching for a rhino club, and he was so
surprised that he ran away.

As I prepared to go down to the Customs House to
register my guns, I was met on the veranda by my boy,
and he was carrying my Express. By some mischievous
devilry he had walked right through the Customs House
with it, while the officers were debating the regulations
with me. I told Monsuri that I would probably need his
help, and I took the gun and went down to the House.
I explained the situation to the Kommandant.

His face went red, and the red became purple. He
sent off a file of askaris to find the boy, and he looked
at me, licked his lips, and thought of the words in his
mouth, and ignored me.

I waited an hour in the Customs House, staring at
a large oil painting of the Kaiser, while the Germans
clicked up and down, the grass fan moving above them,
and the air growing tenser. The askaris came back and
said that they had been unable to find my boy. The
Kommandant swore at them, he slapped their faces and
kicked them from the office.

He looked at me, and I was glad that Monsuri came
in then.

The Germans must have owed him a lot of money,

for he spoke to the Kommandant as I have never heard
a non-European speak to a German. He hectored them
in their own fashion, and fat though he was, he had
tremendous dignity. I paid my two hundred rupees on
each gun. My boy came out of hiding with a sly grin,
and we prepared to depart.

I bought pack donkeys, hired porters from Monsuri, and gratefully accepted his gift of two white muscat riding donkeys. I rode eastward and Monsuri stood
on his veranda waving to me, the tinkling musical box
clutched to his belly. From the lattice of his zenana the
dark eyes of his hundred wives watched us go.

I went up to Ikoma, and it was no longer the stock-
aded outpost I had known when they dug my grave
there years before. It was still very German, however.
I was told to pitch my tent in a compound of prickly
pear where an askari stood on guard with rifle and bayo-
net. I went to greet Antonies, who was now running the
store for Monsuri, and I was pleasantly haggling over
his price for ivory when in came Hoonan and Saunders.

They were in rags and bearded, and the starch had
gone out of Hoonan. He said nothing but sat at the bar
with his head on his arms. Saunders told me that their
camp had been burned out. They had nothing but what
was left of the clothes they were wearing. I asked Antonies to give them each a bottle of beer, and that was
perhaps not a wise thing to do, for the beer brought
back Hoonan's courage.

I took Saunders back to my tent and he got drunk
sullenly on my whisky. He said that Hoonan had been
drunk all the way up from Muanza. He had raided na-

tive villages for food, abducted girls, and this the natives
had let him do because they were afraid of the Germans. Saunders seemed surprised that he and Hoonan
were still alive. He hoped that he would never see
Hoonan alive again.

He said this several times, and then he went down
with fever.

Hoonan drank all the beer that Antonies allowed
him on credit. When that ended, he broke into the German officers' quarters and stole two bottles of whisky.
With one in each hand he walked up and down in front
of the store saying he was going to kill me, a big red
bear of a man, drunk and bad in his drunkenness.

He threw away an empty bottle and went to the
compound, but finding me away, he took my elephant
gun and loaded it.

I saw him from Antonies' store, standing in the
moonlight with his feet astride, his back to us, a bottle
in one hand, the gun in the other. He could have shot
me. I believe he would have shot me if he had seen me,
and I was tired. I was very tired of Hoonan.

I went up behind him, and I bent down and tugged
at his ankles. He fell on his face, firing both barrels of
the elephant gun. The noise brought out a German sergeant and some askaris, and they took Hoonan into the
fort and kept him there until he was sober.

Like most drunkards, like most men who must
drink and must fight the world because they have not
the courage to fight what is inside them, Hoonan was a
creature of terrible pathos when he was sober. He was
released from the fort at last and he came over to the

compound and sat on my bed with his hands trembling, and he said that the Germans were sending him back to Muanza. This seemed to frighten him. He kept saying that the Germans were sending him back to Muanza. He went over to Saunders and took his arm, and told him this. Saunders shook the arm away and turned his back.

Hoonan stood there, and I have seen few men look so lonely, and I was suddenly sorry for him without liking him. I walked off, and when I turned, I saw that he had picked up my gun and broken the breech. He said, "It's loaded," the way a man might say, "It's a fine day," without caring one way or the other.

I was fifteen yards from him and I saw him in my tent. He sat down on the bed and put the muzzle of the gun in his mouth quickly, and crouched over it, reaching down to the triggers with his long hands. He did this quickly, and I was too far away to stop him.

Each cartridge for that gun was loaded with eighty grains of cordite, and it had a striking power of two thousand pounds. Hoonan pulled the trigger.

Saunders looked at Hoonan's body and started to cry. I think he was remembering what he had said, that he hoped he would never see Hoonan alive again.

The game laws killed the life of the old ivory hunters and traders. I knew men who had made five thousand pounds in six months from their ivory, some of it got by trading, but most of it brought in by their own guns, and then came the laws which made contraband all ivory but the few tusks permissible on license.

That killed the old hunters, or sent them further into the bush to be poachers. Perhaps Africa had to legislate these men out of existence, although I do not accept the protection of the elephant as a valid reason. No tribe that had its *shambas* repeatedly devastated by elephant would have thought it a valid reason either. And Africa lost something with the passing of the old hunters. They had gone deep into the country, beyond the waterways and the coastal towns, the first Europeans on the heels of the Arabs. If the settlers and the administrators found the natives ready to take a white man's word, it was because the elephant hunters had set an honest standard of integrity. In their way they had prevented East Africa from becoming the bloody cockpit it could easily have become with the inward movement of whites.

I do not put this up as a defense, but as an explanation. When the game laws increased I went poaching. I poached along the German border and got some ironic amusement from outwitting Ol Dutchie. The Baraki and Sukuma were rich in cattle over there on the German side, and would sell them as low as ten rupees a head when the Germans demanded a three-rupee hut tax.

I bought cattle that was smuggled across the border. It had to be smuggled because the Germans put a twenty-rupee head-tax on all cattle crossing. My camp, whether it was one side or the other of the border, was a clearing house for ivory and cattle. The system was complicated. Sometimes I bought cattle from the Baraki or the Sukuma, smuggled them across and sold them to

British settlers for five pounds a head. Sometimes I shot ivory or traded ivory, and sold it for cattle to Arabs or Greeks in German territory, and the cattle I sold once more to British settlers. All of this was very good business, and none of it entirely legal.

I was in camp one morning when a DC called Crampton came in from Kurungu on Lake Victoria. His police surrounded my hut and he told me that I had been shooting elephant without a license and he was going to search my camp for ivory. I was not worried by this—there was no ivory in the camp—but I was worried by the fact that a drive of smuggled cattle was expected in the camp any hour.

Crampton had his Kavirondo police digging the ground all round the camp, and he came up to me with a piece of ivory weighing about six pounds. He wanted to know where I had got it. I asked where had he got it. It was the tusk of a young bull, and by the little runnels the ants had made on it, it must have been buried in the earth for twenty years.

Crampton said, "I shall issue a summons." He marched off to his camp with his police. He was very dignified and very young.

In the afternoon he sent me a chit. Would I care to come over for tea? I went over, and we were as polite as two curates. He wasn't going to issue a summons, he said.

I said I hoped not. He would need more evidence than a twenty-years'-buried tusk. Could I have permission for two of my boys to leave camp?

He said, "Why?" I said, "For things." He said, "No."
And I wondered how long it would be before the cattle
drive came in and Crampton asked more questions.
Such as, had I paid for them with ivory?

We went on drinking tea and exchanging polite-
nesses. He said that to stop the illicit trade in ivory the
Government was prepared to buy all ivory at four
rupees a pound. I said I would be happy to advise all
natives to take their ivory in to Kurungu. He said that
wasn't quite what he had meant.

Still my cattle did not come. We went shooting
next day, and Mr. District Commissioner Crampton was
very wise and very suspicious. He stayed very close to
me, and listened when I spoke to my boys. But when
we raised a roan antelope he shot it, and went after it,
and I managed to tell a Lumbwa to get away and warn
the cattle drive.

Crampton had made his kill, and was delighted,
and it was a good kill, except that he thought the antelope was a waterbuck. I did not tell him. His boys
brought in the head and the skin and Crampton stood
first on one foot and then on the other to admire it.

I asked him what sort of hunting license he had.
He said a Public Servant's ten-pound license.

I smiled at him. I said, "You ought to summons
yourself, because that's a roan antelope and you are
allowed only two on a fifty-pound license."

We laughed together, but nobody feels so bad
about breaking the law as a man paid to uphold it, and
for all his laughter Crampton felt very badly indeed,
and unhappy that I should know. He struck camp and

went back to Kurungu, and my cattle came in three hours after he had gone.

There was Peffer. He was a nondescript often found in Africa then; the country supported them as it supported its natural parasites. I met him in the Belgian Congo before I went home to have the doctors remove some small shot that had entered my appendix by way of a guinea fowl. Peffer had been in jail, put there by the captain of a German cargo boat, of which Peffer had been an indifferent engineer. The charge was a vague one of mutiny. But when Peffer came out of jail, ragged, dirty and unshaven, I felt a weak sympathy for him, and left him in charge of my guns and my equipment and my dog, Ginger, until I came back from England.

I came back with a motor launch. I wanted a boat that would take me up the Congo and its reaches. I got her in Weybridge and she was beautiful, flat-bottomed, sixty-five feet from stem to stern, and with a beam of nine feet six inches. I took out her engines, which were too weak for the eight-knot currents of the Congo, and I equipped her with a Thorneycroft engine that had been in a lifeboat. I put a searchlight in her bows so that I could see elephant crossing the Congo at night. And I wish I had never bought her, for all her beauty.

She went adrift at Greenwich while I was waiting for her to be loaded on an Elder Dempster liner, and it cost me ten pounds to have her salvaged. The liner ran into foul weather in Biscay, and the launch broke free from her lashings and stove in her port side. When

I got to Matadi, I found that she had been insured against total loss only, and I had to pay for the repairs myself.

The railway men said they would not take her up to Kinchassa. They said she was too long to get round the curves, but I talked them into taking her at my risk. She was always at my risk. On the way to Kinchassa the axle of the railway truck caught fire and scorched the launch on the starboard side. She went back into Lever's yard for repairs, and some crazy native released the brake on a railway coach which ran down and knocked the launch off the slips, damaging her screw.

Finally I got to Kinchassa, and there was Peffer, all grins and beard, ready to be my engineer. I told him to get the launch ready for a river trip and I went up country and soothed my irritation by hunting.

I got back to Thysville to find two letters waiting for me, and they were both about Peffer. While I was in England, he had tried to sell my rifles and equipment, and the British Consul wrote to say that he had stepped in just in time to stop the sale. The second letter was from the indignant manager of Lever's shipyard. Would I please get Peffer off his property? The man was a thief and a drunk.

I took the next train to Kinchassa and found Mr. Peffer in a third-rate Portuguese hotel, where he had been enjoying credit on the strength of his claim that he was my partner.

The place looked like a film set. There were Germans, Russians, Italians, Portuguese, Spaniards and

Greeks, with Peffer entertaining them generously. He waved to me and invited me to join him and his friends. I picked him up by the shirt-front and I said that I hoped he would put as much of Africa as he could between us. It was a large country, but it was rapidly getting too small for both Peffer and Jordan. He was fired, I said. I wasn't quite sure what job he had with me, but he was fired from it. He was also fired from whatever job he had told his creditors he had with John Alfred Jordan.

The crowd rose up. Everyone, it seemed, was Peffer's creditor, and in several languages it was pointed out that if Peffer could not pay his debts, Jordan should pay them.

I sat him down among them and left.

The next morning I received a court summons, informing me that Monsieur Peffer was suing me for unpaid wages. I went up to Leopoldville to fight the case, and there was Peffer with a cloud of witnesses. But I won the case, and as I left the court Peffer trotted up to me. Breathing the last memory of the whisky he had obtained on my credit, he said that justice in the Belgian Congo was obviously a fraud, and that he proposed to rectify this by setting fire to the launch.

I thanked him. I said I would be sleeping aboard that night with an elephant gun, and should I miss him with this, which was unlikely, there was still my dog, Ginger, which had not learned to love him during my absence.

I sat up the night waiting for Peffer, but he did not come. The last I heard of him was that he was under arrest. He had killed a native, and for this I think he was hanged.

But perhaps he put a curse on the launch, for I had no luck with her. I loved her, and I wanted her to share the Congo with me. It was a great and magnificent river. Big stern-wheelers creamed its red waters, a hot and green Africa embraced it, and there was room on it for a man to expand his lungs.

Nobody else loved my launch. When you tried to start her engines, they would backfire with a venom that nearly broke the arm of one of Lever's engineers. The backfire also knocked one of my Mouwazie boys into the water, so I hired a powerful Turk called Panhard, who looked at the engine and sneered. The handle caught him on the throat and laid him out. He recovered and said that he would stay in the crew, but he would not handle the engine.

When she was fit, I had her towed upriver, made fast to the port side of a tug. The skipper of the tug said he was French, but nothing he ever said was true. He had already lost one ship, and this tug was his first command under Lever's flag, and almost his last, for her wood-pile caught fire and dropped hot embers over my launch which was carrying fifty gallons of gasoline and three cases of cartridges. At that the skipper might have been French, for French was the language he spoke when he lost his head. But we managed to push the burning wood overboard on the starboard side, and I prayed that this would be all. The following forenoon a gale blew up, tore tug and launch from the moorings, and took both, lashed fast together, downriver to a sandbank.

We got off the next morning, and when I asked the skipper to point out our position on the chart he happily confessed that he couldn't read a chart, but that we were probably within two days of Kwilo; he had never been up the Congo this far. At Kwilo we hit hard currents, and instead of signaling Full Speed, the skipper thought it advisable to stop altogether and we nearly capsized in midstream. I parted from him with great relief.

Up there, along the Congo, was a happy land for ivory. I was the only Englishman there, but there were French and Portuguese as well, and the Belgians had askaris patrolling the river and its tributaries to catch us. Two Portuguese were our middlemen. They ran a trading store and operated a twenty-ton steamer, dirty white and very old, and this took our ivory over to the French bank where it was sold. The skipper of the steamer was a blade called Figuarido, a twentieth-century freebooter with the blood of Magellan in him. He would bring the steamer into the bank near my camp, and he would stand on deck and bargain with me, dirty, greasy, grinning. He was a good fellow, and always gave me a good price, sometimes throwing in a case of champagne or a demijohn of red wine. I never saw Figuarido ashore, always he was on his steamer.

Yet one day he was brought ashore, and in a sad way. Askaris ambushed him from the bank, and when he laughed at the order to put in, they opened fire.

They shot his helmsman away from the wheel, and his steamer went crazily on to a sandbank where there were more askaris. That was the end of Figuarido, the freebooter. With him ended the only means of disposing of my ivory.

When I was at Ikoma in German East, a dapper young lieutenant called Fischer sold me a Wilkinson .500 Express and two hundred cartridges for twenty pounds. It was a good gun and a good bargain, but I was a fool and forgot to register it with the Germans. I thought Fischer would have done this, and perhaps he had, although it would have made no difference.

Not that I liked Fischer. He was the sort of German you found along the borders of German East before 1914, and it was not until the war that you realized why they were there. His story was that he was an officer in the German regular army, with a year's leave to go shooting in Africa. He did most of his shooting along the British border, and he did more map-making than shooting, which may explain why he had no use for the Express.

He lived well (it was his whisky that Hoonan stole). He had two house servants and a gunbearer, a splendid Nyassa boy called Mohammed, who had been an askari for ten years. While I was at Ikoma, Mohammed ran away from Fischer and asked me to employ him. He said the only wages Fischer had paid had been with the lash. He was brave and he was loyal, and these were characteristics the Germans rarely found in the natives, though they always got obedience.

I did some shooting with that Express—rhino, buffalo, elephant—and then the luck ran out. My leg, the
leg of the Boer bullet, and the Kisi spear, and the
mamba bite, turned malignant and crippled me. Where
I went, I rode, on a docile muscat donkey. I went out
one morning and killed a Jackson hartebeest with a
long-range shot between the eyes that made me feel
good, and it was always when I was feeling that good
that something bad happened.

This time my bearer had overloosened the girth
strap, and when the gentle muscat smelt lion in the bush
it bolted. It went down an incline, and the saddle
slipped up to its neck and round, and threw me. I heard
the snick as my shoulder went out, and then a great
rush of sickening pain. One of my Lumbwa came up
and knelt on me, and he smiled at me. He took the
shoulder in his hands and forced it back as you might
reset a book on a bookshelf.

It put my arm in a sling for a month, and I wandered about the country in a foul temper, firing an elephant gun with one hand from my left shoulder, which
showed the sort of humor I was in.

The shoulder improved, and as it improved the
goodness came back to me, and that ought to have been
enough to warn me. I was stalking lion when I came
over a rise and saw a big camp in the valley below.
There was a flag on a post—the red, white, and black
and eagle of Imperial Germany. So there should have
been, for when I got down there I discovered that His
Excellency Baron von Dernberg, German Colonial Secretary, a dozen of his train, a hundred soldiers and three

hundred porters, were on a grand tour of the colony.

They had been following the Anglo-German border, and no doubt Lieutenant Fischer's little maps were very useful.

Von Dernberg was a good-natured man and welcomed me. It was a pity he was not aware of the irony of shaking hands with an ivory poacher. The irony was not lost on his captain of askaris, Schultz, a leatherfaced man who kept slapping his boots with a whip and staring at me. Von Dernberg wanted me to lend them a guide to Ikoma, so I lent them two Lumbwa, and gave the Secretary some skins, leopard skins, which he had admired.

It took the caravan over two hours to trail past my camp, and they left me holding a box of cigars which Von Dernberg had given me. I was smoking one happily as the tail of the safari passed, twenty askaris under Schultz. He stopped his soldiers there and came up to me, feet astride, holding his crop behind him. My papers? My licenses?

He leafed through them, and then he saw the Express I had bought from Fischer. Where was its registration note? I said I had none, and he told an askari to pick up the gun. I explained, as patiently as I could, that I had exhausted my light ammunition, that the Express was the only usable gun I had. How was I to protect my livestock and feed my carriers if he took it away? I would pay the registration fee to him if he would leave me the gun.

He looked at me with his pale blue eyes and he began to describe for me his view of my personal ap-

pearance, my history and my ancestry. I replied as un-
favorably as I could about his own, and he hit his thigh
with the crop and went off with my gun.

I brooded on this for an hour, and my Lumbwa
pretended that they were not curious to know what the
Bwana Mkuba would do about this.

I struck camp and went after the Germans. I found
them, spread out again under the German flag, and Von
Dernberg was asleep under the netting. I sat outside his
tent until he woke up, and he smiled and said he was
pleased to see me again, would I take him to shoot
some buffalo? Schultz was waiting, listening, so I
thought that a buffalo shoot would be as private a con-
versation with the Secretary as I could hope for. We
shot no buffalo, but every time I mentioned the gun
the Secretary talked about British East. There was much
he wanted to know about British East, and there was
little he learned from me, and in the end he capitulated
with a smile and told Schultz to give me back the gun.

I went back to Shirati, registered the gun and left
it there. There I met an agent of Hagenbeck who
wanted me to collect young buffalo, so I went back
into the forest, which means that I went back into the
Schultz patrol area. I killed buffalo, I killed badly,
something was wrong with my nerves. I fired eighteen
rounds of .303 before I managed to kill an old bull, and
this had never happened to me before. Anyway, I was
supposed to be capturing buffalo calves, not shooting
old bulls. I had two rounds left. I put one boy on skinning the bull, and sent the other, Abdullah, back to
camp for more ammunition.

He returned two hours later. He could not talk at first. Then he said that he had seen Ol Dutchie raiding my camp. It was Schultz. Abdullah had lain in the bush, and he watched while the askaris ripped up my tent, emptied my boxes, packed all my equipment on their donkeys. An askari dragged Abdullah from the bush, and Schultz had had him flogged.

I ran back to the camp. I found strips of canvas and a kettle. Two of my boys came out of the bush, and I told them to go out and find the way Ol Dutchie had gone. They went out, but they did not come back, and I could not blame them, for I could win no fight against Schultz. Abdullah went in the night and I was alone.

I stood up alone, with my rifle and my two rounds, with my kettle and my strips of ten canvas, and I swore that I would find Schultz and kill him. I thought of how I would kill him, and each death I thought of was too compassionate for my hatred. And I knew that he wanted me to follow him, and that it would not be me who killed him, but he who killed me. He had everything I owned, my equipment, my papers, my photographs. I had a kettle, a rifle and two rounds. And my boys had run from me because they knew I was already dead.

I had eighty miles to walk to Kericho, the first British post I could reach, and I had to walk with one swollen foot in a self-made sandal.

I could walk the eighty miles, or I could sit there and die. But there is great strength in hatred. I drank from the stream. I filled the kettle and took it in my left hand, and with my rifle in the right I began to walk.

I walked, and this I wonder at now, I walked thirty-five miles to where the Naluba Hills broke out of the ground. Every mile I walked I stopped to count those two rounds of .303.

I was delirious at sunset, but I made a fire and killed my hunger with cigarettes. I slept and I awoke, and I unbound my foot and rubbed the dried blood from the bandage and rewound it.

As I sat there, trying to remember the trail to the Mara River, a bush cracked behind me, there was a sudden throttled bleat. I dragged myself toward it, shouting. I saw a leopard swerve over the body of an impala, and back from it snarling. I threw stones at it, shouting, screaming, until it swung its tail and went. The impala wasn't dead, and I cut its throat without pity. I cut out the liver and ate it raw. As I ate, the leopard returned and spat at me from the brush. I took a leg from the impala and went on a mile, where I lit a fire, and cooked the leg, and drank from my kettle, and felt good again.

I remember little of the walk, except the growing heat of my leg, how the foot hurt every time I put it down until it hurt no longer and I knew that it was as bad as it could be. And I told myself that this was the leg the Kisi had speared, and this was the leg the drunken doctor had wanted to amputate. I said, "If they had taken it off, Jordan, you wouldn't have been able to walk this far, would you?" The joke kept me going for a few miles, which proves it was not that bad a joke.

I got to the Mara. It is a fast river, rising high and hurrying through tall bluffs to the lake, and when I got to it, it was in flood. The trees along its banks were full of monkeys, blue, gray, black and white, some of them as small as kittens, and they hung from the vines by their tails and shrieked at me. I lay in a glade among the flowers and looked at the river, and I crawled down to it and let it rush coolly over my burning foot. Then I tried leapfrogging from stone to stone, one leg only, until I lost my balance and had to put my other foot down. The pain of it went up to my chest and threw me in the water.

I got to the bank and lay with my mouth in the mud, and I swore at Schultz. I swore at him because the river had taken the leg of the impala, and there could be nothing as bad as its loss.

I unwound the bandage from my foot and gazed at its ugly beauty. I built a fire at dusk and sat by it, putting on brush, afraid to sleep. A young lioness swerved into the light and snarled when I shouted at her. In the morning I believed that I knew the country, but I was ready to believe that whether it were true or not. I believed that I was within two miles of a Lumbwa village, and I looked at my foot and touched it with my finger and felt the pain out of all proportion to the lightness of that touch, yet I believed I could walk that two miles.

I walked some of it, with the rifle as a crutch, and some of it I crawled, pulling myself on my belly. I played cunning tricks on my mind, telling myself that it was not two miles I had to go, but a hundred yards to that tree, or fifty to that bush. And sometimes I lay still on the ground and called myself a liar, because it was really two miles to that village.

At last I pulled myself up to a stump and lit my final cigarette, and I knew that this was as far as I was going to go. A topi-hartebeest came out of the bush two hundred yards away, two hundred miles away, and I shot it, a wasteful, futile shot, but perhaps I shot it because it was fine and alive and I believed I was going to die there with my back against a tree stump. The .303 took it in the flank and it was gone, and I was sorry that I had only wounded it and could not follow and kill it and save it from pain. But the sound of the gun jerked my intelligence and taught me something I would have known instinctively had the fire not been burning up my leg to my head. I fired the last round into the air and hoped the Lumbwa would hear.

They heard and they came at dusk, as I was sitting there unable to make a fire and knowing that without a fire I would not be alive at dawn. The Lumbwa came to find the hunter who had fired the shots and perhaps beg meat from him. They were Mataia's people and they took me to him. He swore at his wives and a sheep was slaughtered. He sent a runner forty miles to Kericho, his best runner, carrying a cleft stick with my note in it, and a red rag tied to the stick to show that he was an important messenger.

The note was to Alidan Vissram, the Hindu storekeeper, and it listed the supplies I wanted, and I was no longer a man who expected to die in the bush, and who would have died in the bush if Schultz's plan had worked. I was a hunter again, with supplies coming from Alidan Vissram, and a very great hatred for Schultz.

I tried to get satisfaction out of the Germans. I wrote long letters to the Colonial Governor, saying, as politely as I could, that the Kommandant up at Shirati, one Schultz, was a pig, and I would kill him did I not think it more civilized to make this complaint. The Germans acknowledged my letters stiffly, and they did nothing else. So I decided that if they were not going to get my equipment back for me, then I would take their ivory.

I went up to the Shirati country; if I had to poach I would poach in Schultz's garden. I got many fine tusks and I sold them to two Arabs called Akeeda and Amboga. They paid me in cattle which I sold to British settlers for handsome prices. There were many elephants there that year. They had come over from the Kisi highlands in British East, driven away by the sportsmen who were threshing about in the forests getting material for their books. I knew that if the Germans caught me, they would shoot me, and they would send a letter of regret to the British authorities saying that they had found Herr Jordan breaking the law, and that he had been shot while attempting to escape. But they did not catch me. I put scouts on the high tops of the Murati hills, and they watched the country for me, and behind their vigilance I shot elephants as I wished.

That was a good summer. I shot an old bull whose right tusk weighed 112 pounds, and the other would have been almost as great had it not been broken, but between them they must have made many piano keys. It took my boys two hours to cut out the tusks and bury them where they could stay until I got them through to Akeeda and Amboga.

There was a Masai chief called Tamani who had brought his people over to live in German East, and he acted as my agent with the Arabs, taking my ivory to them and accepting the cattle on my behalf. I got sixteen head of cattle for those tusks of the old bull, and I sold the cattle for nearly one hundred pounds. With such good fortune I began to take a more tolerant attitude toward Schultz. In four months I made nearly a thousand pounds.

Then the Arabs failed to send cattle for my last delivery of ivory. They sent word that they had run out of cattle, and the look on Tamani's face when he told me indicated that he did not believe the story any more than I did. When did Arabs ever run out of cattle?

I decided to go in to Fort Ikoma and find out for myself. If I had not been feeling so good about the ivory, and if my foot were not healthy again, I would not have taken so foolish a risk. There were at least two dozen people in Ikoma who would recognize me. I shaved off my mustache, and put on a dirty white gown and red fez, and went to Ikoma, hoping that I looked like an Arab. I stopped in the bush outside the fort and sent my boy in to Antonies, and I sent an *elmoran* with him too. The warrior came back and said that it was safe, but when I got to the Greek's store, an askari had the boy by the shoulder and was questioning him. He called to me in Swahili, and I mumbled back at him, and he looked at me and then released the boy and went away.

Antonies chuckled greasily, and complimented me on my appearance. He kept pretending I was really an Arab and swearing at me, and then when he had exhausted his joke he told me that the Germans were looking for me and that this time they were determined to find me. My Arabs knew this, and they had decided to keep the ivory I had sent them and tell the Germans where I was. Antonies smiled again and said, "You Arabs are all alike."

When I returned to Tamani's village, there were two drunken askaris in a hut. They had come to enquire about me and Tamani had refused to answer questions until they had drunk with him, and he had gone on pouring honey beer into them until they were unconscious. While they slept, I took my boys and left, making camp about a mile from the British border.

I was trailing a wounded lioness two days later when I came on the marks of a camp. There were prints of nailed boots in the soil, and a little pyramid of empty beer bottles. Up the trail I found a Wanderobo and he told me that six German officers, fifty askaris, and two hundred Marti tribesmen were out looking for me. It was only his opinion, of course, but it could not be long before they found me.

When my boys heard this they panicked. Some of them ran for the border that night, and probably the Germans got them before they could cross. I managed to calm the others, but that night I saw the Germans' campfires surrounding me. The red blotches formed a

large semicircle to the east. The left flank rested on the
German border. The center was five miles *into* British
territory, and the right flank was on the edge of the
Marti hills. There is a clear drop of several hundred feet
onto the Amala Plain on the other side of the hills. The
Germans had me pinned up against the border, inside
my own country geographically, but very much inside
their cordon.

If I retreated, it would be back into German East;
and if I tried to move north or south, they could outflank me. The only weak part of their cordon was that
drop down the escarpment to the Amala Plain.

I told the boys to bury my ivory and mark the spot.
I went over to Tamani's village, and the Masai began to
sound drums and blow horns by way of a welcome until
I quietened them. I told Tamani that Ol Dutchie was
out there in the bush, the Masai could see the fires.
Tamani said he had seen them. They were looking for
me, I admitted, but they would also be angry with the
Masai and would take sheep and cattle and burn huts
in their anger. I said the Masai must know a way down
this escarpment, and Tamani said this was so.

We went down together, down a path as wide as a
window ledge at times, and I rode down it on a donkey
for my foot was bad again. The Masai brushed out the
trail behind us, and I was glad that it was dark and I
could not see.

We camped at the foot of the escarpment, and
shortly after dawn the Masai who had been brushing
out our spoor padded in to say that Ol Dutchie was
close. He had Wanderobo trackers with him, which I

should have expected, and these clever little men had found a way down the cliffs.

I threw water on the fire. I told my boys to make for the Naluba Hills, and with my bearer I crossed over the Amala River and hid in the trees. Tamani's village went away quickly in a cloud of dust.

As I waited, Ol Dutchie came out of the trees on the other side of the Amala. It was a small scouting party, one officer on a mule, fifteen askaris, and a score of Marti tribesmen. They found our spoor by the river, but the German, perhaps feeling bad about being this far into British territory, would not cross the river. He stared across the water, while his Marti sat down on their heels and waited. My donkey suddenly appreciated the humor of the situation and began to bray ribaldly. I clamped its jaws with my hand. The Marti stood up and three or four of them went into the water toward me.

The German sat very still. I could almost see him working out the problem in his mind, and then he knew he could not pursue me indefinitely into British East, and he called off the Marti and went back into the trees.

I still wanted the cattle which the Arabs owed me, so I went to see Tamani again. He was a cunning and delightful man, with an ironic sense of humor. We worked out a plan between us. He moved back into German East and sent a runner to Shirati to find the Arabs. Tamani, said the runner, had two tusks so heavy that four men would find them heavy to lift. Were the Arabs interested? The Arabs were interested, but they were not interested in meeting Bwana Jordan. Bwana

Jordan, said the runner, had been driven from the country by Ol Dutchie, and was skulking in fear beyond the Mara.

"We will come," said the Arabs, "and we will bring cattle for the tusks."

I waited five or six miles outside Tamani's village, and I waited ten days before his messenger came and told me that the Arabs were now in the Masai village with forty cattle and two donkeys. Tamani had not closed the deal for the tusks, but was still bargaining, and he had not put the Arabs' cattle with his own herd, but kept them separate on a hill slope where his warriors were guarding them.

I made a forced march and arrived in the Masai village an hour after noon. I told four of my boys to drive the Arabs' cattle into the bush, and then I walked into the village carrying a .303. I sat down before Tamani's hut with the rifle across my knee, and gave the Arabs a good morning. Tamani grinned.

Where, I asked, were the cattle the Arabs owed me?

They shifted their eyes and poked at the dust. Times were bad. They had not bought in cattle for many weeks. Ol Dutchie was angry with them for trading with me. I understood, of course?

I said that I understood, but that it was hard to see why they had come to Tamani's village.

They said that Tamani was their friend, and that a man found pleasure in talking and eating with his friends.

I said that this was true, and that in business as

well as in friendship there could be no trust without honesty.

And so we traded innuendoes until one of Tamani's herdsmen came up. He was a superb actor. He rolled his eyes and went down on his knees, and Tamani looked at him sternly, and cursed him, and told him to speak clearly. The herdsman said that while he watched the Arabs' cattle, he had slept, and for this he was ashamed and dishonored, and that while he slept the cattle had strayed into the bush and were lost.

The Arabs looked at Tamani, and they looked at me, and they looked at my rifle, and they were very unhappy Arabs.

✳ T W E L V E ✳

Even Gorillas Will Cry

You kill a gorilla, said Jordan, and you think it is an animal you have killed, but it is really your cousin, a man walking on two feet, and when you kill one, its friends grieve over its body.

Not that you can feel sentimental about them, the way you might about an impala buck, which does not walk on two legs but has eyes like a gentle cow. There is nothing gentle about a gorilla. It has large tusks and cheek teeth, and terrible ugliness in the black, leather nasal fold that runs to the margin of the upper lip. It has broad, short and thick hands, and its fingers and toes are partly webbed. It is something out of your nightmares. It is the eternal mockery of our common origin, and I never killed one with pleasure.

Even gorillas will cry, or get very close to human grief.

Along the Congo an old native once came into my camp and asked me if I would frighten away a colony of chimpanzees that was raiding his village gardens. Because I knew that natives are deliberately vague about the genus of apes, I said, "Truly chimpanzee?"

And he said, "Truly, Bwana, *soko.*"

We found the trail from the village, where the

banana trees had been torn, and I knew as soon as I began that this was not the work of chipanzees, and perhaps the old native did too, but had been afraid that I would not come if he told me the truth.

The truth was sitting in the forest ahead of us when I parted the vines, three gorillas in a circle, their tight scalp hair erect, their black shoulders bowed. They were sitting there banging their wrists on the earth and grunting, and there was another stalking about as if he were dummy in some simian hand of bridge. I looked my disgust at the old native, and he smiled shyly.

I did not want to kill the gorilla, but I was happy to see them, for I hoped that somewhere was a young one that I could capture and sell to Hagenbeck.

The big fellow stalking the circle was tremendous, with yellow skin beneath the hairs on his chest. There was a blue sheen on his shoulders and back, and the naked flesh of his muzzle looked like a rubber mask. He had a big cooper's barrel for his body, and long, swinging arms. He looked into the forest and flexed his lips over his tusks, and his black eyes had that wild, unhappy desperation you see in gorillas.

"*Piga*, Bwana!" said my guide softly. I shook my head. The old man looked very unhappy, and then uncomfortable. If I were not going to shoot, what was he doing there?

The big male drew himself up to seven feet, hit himself on the chest with a blow that would have knocked down an ox, and he whoofed. The others stood up quickly from their game of cards, and they held their heads to one side cunningly. They were listening away from us, over to the other side of the glade, and the big male whoofed again.

The trees crashed and a bull elephant pushed his way out amiably. He had a sweep of white tusks that curved magnificently, and he raised his trunk and blared at the gorillas. They snarled, and the female screamed, and all of them backed away, with their lips pulled from their teeth.

Instinct is a compelling thing, and I could not let that tusker go. His tusks must have weighed over a hundred pounds each. I gave him one barrel of the Express. I must have forgotten all about the gorillas, or else the size and importance of them were nothing against this great bull. The shot went in behind his ear to the brainpan, and he went down with a crash.

The gorillas screamed. Two of them clambered over the elephant's body like children, but the big male and his mate came toward us obliquely. I aimed at him, to bring him down or at least frighten them away from us, but they swerved, and the Express bullet caught the female in the head and killed her.

The big male stopped, and the others came back over the dead bull, and they stood about the dead female. They got down beside her, and they began to stroke her body. They made odd, soothing sounds, crooning, and the sound of them was like weeping. The face of the old man beside me went gray.

The gorillas grieved over the body for ten minutes, and then they picked it up gently, and carried it away through the trees.

I wanted to follow, but I knew that if I did, I

would have to kill another should they discover me,
and at that moment I never wanted to kill a gorilla
again. But in the morning I went out with three boys,
following the spoor until we found the dead female.

Her friends had laid her at the foot of a tree, and
they had broken down the bushes about her, and they
had covered her with branches.

In the Kivu district there was once quite a large
colony of gorillas, and perhaps there still is. They were
not the biggest gorillas you could find in Africa—smaller,
that is, than those you found among the cedar and
juniper of the Ituri forest—but they were big enough
to look at without bars between you both.

I was at Stanleyville when I heard that the Belgians were abandoning an experimental rubber and
coffee plantation at La Romeo, and since I had the
land-buying fever then, I thought I would go up and
see if the plantation were worth buying. I was living
there in one of the brick huts when a native came in
and said there was a large tusker in the forest. I went
out after it and it led us for fifteen miles before I was
able to kill it. It was not a good kill, it was a very bad
kill, or else that tusker had an evil spirit, for I fired
twenty-nine shells into it before it came down. And
when they were fired, I had no more ammunition.

I was too far from the plantation to return that
night, so I stayed in the native village. It was a noisy
night. The natives fired guns and beat drums, and in the
morning I was told that the village had been under siege

from a tribe of chimpanzees. I asked the natives to go out and get me a young one, alive, for I still had ideas of getting one for Hagenbeck, but they smiled, and suggested that the Bwana come along.

We were out for two hours, and then I saw something pacing about in a glade ahead, and it was far too big for a chimpanzee, who can be big enough. This was a grizzled male gorilla in a very bad temper.

The natives were armed with brass-bound muzzle-loaders. When they saw this gorilla, their little faces twisted with hatred. I would have been happier to let the thing go; I had no ammunition, and I did not trust their guns. I said, "Leave it. Come away."

But two of them stood up and fired at the gorilla. I saw the scrap iron snapping at the branches all round the gorilla, and I saw its skin shudder as some pieces hit, the way a horse will twitch to be rid of flies. Then it roared, and flailed the air with its arms. Three other gorillas that had been chatting in the brush, rose up quickly and padded away, but the old male went over to the offensive.

It caught one of the natives while the man was trying to recharge his muzzle-loader, and it picked him up by the throat and squeezed, and I heard the crack of the neck breaking. Another native ran in with a squeal, and beat the gorilla with the butt of his musket. The gorilla took the gun away from him and smashed his skull with it.

The others closed in, shouting, and they fired a volley. The gorilla was now bleeding on its chest and face, and one eye had been torn away. The other was red. It is an old simile, but it glowed like a coal, a black coal sunk in fire, with the ebony of the pupil and the blood of the reddened rim. The gorilla's mouth opened to shriek.

When it caught a native in its hands, it slew quickly and dropped the body. The natives darted in and fired, and dodged away, and the gorilla stood on its bow legs and died magnificently in the blue smoke of gunpowder, roaring, snatching, killing, until there were six bodies at its feet.

At last three natives went within the gorilla's reach, pushing the muzzles of their muskets against the body as they fired. One had his arm pulled out as the gorilla went down, and the others swarmed out, screaming, spitting at the gorilla and firing their guns into its body long after it was dead. They left it there.

It was just over six feet tall. Its chest measured eighty-six inches, and it must have weighed nearly six hundred pounds.

I was following an elephant in the Ituri Forest when I saw a gorilla kill a leopard.

I found the leopard first. It had snatched a young monkey and was eating the entrails when I drove it away with a bullet that broke its right hind leg. I trailed it, and the trail was easy. There was very little underbrush in the trees and much blood on the earth. But for an animal on three legs only it made good speed, and I followed at the double. It went for an abandoned village, where the empty huts were throttled by vine, and where, standing in the path of the leopard, was a man.

I shouted to him to beware of the leopard, and then I saw that this was not a man but a gorilla.

Neither gorilla nor leopard would give way in that narrow street. The gorilla pulled back its lips and roared, and the leopard went down on its belly, shuffled, and leaped at the gorilla's head. The gorilla caught it by the throat with a casual, upward, holding sweeping of its arm, and it held the threshing cat there while it slowly wrenched at each limb.

The leopard died bravely, but it died, and the gorilla tossed it on the ground and walked on it, pounded with great feet until it was satisfied. It dragged the leopard by the tail to the foot of a castor oil tree, and left it there. It scratched the blood on its chest, and went away.

I went over to the leopard and prodded its body with my rifle. It was as soft and as unresisting as a feather pillow.

I bought a young gorilla once, from a Portuguese engineer on a Congo stern-wheeler. The engineer thought it was a chimp. He had the gorilla in the bows of his ship, in a cage, and the gorilla crouched in this little space like a black cloud of sorrow. I bought him, and with him I bought an equally unhappy young chimp and a young leopard.

The engineer said I could have the gorilla for a thousand francs, but first he was going to tame it. He was going upriver and he would have the animal tamed

before he returned. But when he came back, the gorilla
was dead. He had died the way a human will sometimes
die, by deciding not to live.

I bought and sold many chimpanzees. I had one
that went down with fever and would have died, but
I gave him injections of quinine, and I gave him milk
and eggs and nursed him like a baby, and although my
young leopard bit a piece from his ear, he lived.

There are supposed to be eight principal families
of chimpanzees, but the three I was familiar with had
not been classified then. They lived in the Congo forests,
and the Mabuti pygmies were said to be their cousins.
In fact, the other natives, who thought pygmies let
down the tone of the continent, claimed that you could
not tell where a chimpanzee left off and a Mabuti began.

My chimpanzee friends belonged to the Stanleyville sept, and these are believed to be the biggest and
the most human, if you have no objection to the word.
They can be as tall as young gorilla, and when they are
adult they cannot be kept in captivity. Like the gorillas,
they can will themselves to death.

Even a young chimp will go on hunger strike when
you catch him. But after a while he gives in, and his
disagreeable mood thaws into embarrassing affection.

I have seen as many as thirty chimpanzee in the
Ituri, and natives have told me that they have seen colonies of more than fifty, but this I do not believe. Even
with a rifle you have, at the best, even odds with a
disgruntled chimp. When he goes up to fight he has
the pink face of a senile old man, and the superb body

of an athlete. He must be killed, if it is killing you are after, with the first shot, for even wounded he will take a gazelle's leap and kill you.

The Stanleyville natives hated chimps. Colonies of them would strip the gardens from end to end, indifferent to the firing of guns, the shouting, the horns blowing. They ate until they were satisfied, and if they were not satisfied they would move into the village and raid the huts.

My greatest friend was Soko. I captured him when he was young, when I was hunting around Stanleyville, and he refused to eat for three days after I captured him, but sat with his knees under his chin, and his long pink hands over his ridiculous ears. But finally a pot of jam broke down his reserve, and he forgot that I had shot his mother. I had to shoot her. She was five feet two inches tall, and fifty-two inches around the chest, and she was in a bad temper. But when I had shot her, and took Soko from her, I saw that the skin on her face was almost as pink as a European's. She had mutton-chop whiskers and she looked quite ridiculous, even in death.

Soko forgot her. He learned to use a sewing-machine, to clean his teeth, to sit at table with me. And he loved me so much that he was jealous of every other beast I captured. I once took a fledgling marabout from a nest, and this grew up on the launch with us, finding its own food along the bank. I grew quite fond of it, so Soko wrung its neck.

I took him back to England with me when I went home for the war in 1914. He was enlisted, too, at the recruiting office, but there was not much he could do in the war, so I handed him over to the Philadelphia Zoo.

He was quite human, which, in view of men like Hoonan and Peffer and Schultz, may not be a compliment.

✳ T H I R T E E N ✳

The Jablanket-Machoies

I once met some leopards, said Jordan, that walked like men.

One year on the Loita plains the desire to find the Elephant Stone was strong inside me and I let many elephants pass, looking for the tuskless bull that would carry the gem behind his eye socket. I never found him, but I was forced to shoot one big tusker that charged us and I hit him in the lung. He went away through the scrub, blowing a froth of blood that hung on the vines like pink grapes. We tracked his spoor until nightfall.

The night was moonless and uneasy, and I lay awake for most of it, looking beyond the rim of the fire to the darkness, and many times I thought I saw shapes moving there. The only one I saw clearly was a yellow hyena, brushing the earth with its snout, and it came into the firelight and took the foot of my gunbearer in its jaws. The boy awoke and the camp awoke, and the Lumbwa threshed around in the bush with their spears. I called them in, and I told them that I had seen a strange thing, many leopard out there in the bush, and they looked at me in an odd way and said nothing. But

I was puzzled too, for I was sure it had been leopards I had seen, and leopards rarely run in crowds.

We followed the blood-spoor in the morning, westward, and it was a trail I did not much like, for it led toward the hills where the Kisi had been raiding. In two hours we saw vultures hanging, and I knew we had found the tusker. When we came upon it the tusks had gone. My Lumbwa walked about the dead elephant, soft-footed and muttering. I called them and told them that we would pursue the Kisi and recover the tusks.

They stood still and looked at the dust. I asked them whether their blood had turned to water. I asked them whether the Lumbwa were now afraid of the Kisi who were women compared with the Lumbwa. They were still silent, and I told them that the Lumbwa had always been my brothers and I had not believed there could be this weakness in them.

Arab Moina, my bearer, said it had not been the Kisi who stole the tusks, but the *jablanket-machoies,* and when he said it had been the leopard-wizards I laughed at him. My laughing made the Lumbwa more sullen. Arab Moina went to the elephant and pointed his sword at the earth, and suggested that the Bwana see for himself, there was no spoor of man, only the tracks of leopard.

It was the truth. There were no footprints, only the pad-marks of a lioness or a leopard, and many of them. Also I knew that if the Kisi had taken the tusks they would not have left the meat, for the Kisi, if they have no taste for killing elephant, have a great longing for its meat.

I said to Arab Moina, there are no such things as leopard-men.

He said, "Who took the tusks, Bwana?" Which was a question I could not answer.

I said, "Who are the *jablanket-machoies?*"

They were *shitanis*, Bwana. They were devils who were part man and part leopard, and all the evil of man and all the cunning of leopard. Once a month they hunted elephant and hunted man. They carried guns, and they liked to eat women.

I said this was what men dreamed when they had taken too much honey-beer.

It was true, Bwana. Many times had Arab Moina seen their camps in the forest, and the bones of men about the dead fires. There had been a great warrior of the Setick Lumbwa who had been captured by the leopard-men. They had bitten him in the arm and in the shoulder, and had clawed his head the way leopards will.

He broke free from them and ran to his village, and as he ran the leopard-men had fired a musket ball into his arm. Because his people knew him to be a great warrior they believed what he told them. The next day the poison from the claw marks entered his brain, and he walked in the forest, laughing and talking to himself. This had happened many rains before, but there had been much else to prove that the *jablanket-machoies* were real.

I said that if this were so the Lumbwa should follow me and destroy the leopard-men. I called them cowards, but although Arab Moina and the others had

hunted with me many times, none of them would go
further than the body of the elephant.

So I took them away, and we went down toward
the Engabai where the river flows musically and the
heat is less cruel. On the fifth day, needing food and
fresh porters, I went over to a village of the Buragi on
the heights above the river. They had been a happy
and satisfied people, but when I arrived their village
was empty and the elephant grass had come in like the
tide and was growing inside the huts. By the zareba
where the Buragi had kraaled their sheep and goats I
found the skeletons of men.

Arab Moina looked at them and he said, "*Jablanket-
machoies.*"

I said that this was nonsense. I said the village
had been destroyed in a Masai raid, and this was something the Lumbwa had seen many times. Why should
it now be because of the leopard-men, when there were
no such things as leopard-men.

The butterflies were dancing above the ruins of the
huts, and over the abandoned *shambas*, and it was only
by threats that I got the Lumbwa to dig sweet potatoes
from the gardens.

I said we would go up to the Marti on the blue escarpment above the plains, and they would give us food,
but also I was thinking about the leopard-men, and I
was not sure what I was thinking.

We climbed the escarpment slowly, and drums began to sound along the ridge of it before we had climbed
halfway. Arab Moina said that the drums were calling
the old men to a *shauri*. We had been seen, and there

was need for council. The warriors of the Marti were drawn up in a battle line when we topped the escarpment, and they came down on us, crouching behind their black, elliptical shields, their spears moving rhythmically. I spoke to them, and they called out that they had no food. The old chief came, flipping the flies from his face with a lion-hair whisk, and he greeted me amiably for I had killed meat for his tribe during the famine and we were friends. He would not tell me why the drums were beating, why there was need for a great *shauri*, or why his young men were so angry and so frightened, but he looked sideways from his face and invited me to join the council.

After moonrise that evening, fifty old men sat in their blankets about a great fire, including four witch doctors, dressed in their finest bones and skulls and snakeskins, and so worried were they that they forgot to bless me with their traditional sneer.

From the circumlocutionary jargon of the speakers I learned that two days before a message had come to the Marti from the leopard-men, and I could not understand from the drifting, grunting talk how such a message had come, but it demanded that the Marti send two young girls and two young boys to the shallow ford of the Amala, because they were needed as a sacrifice to the leopard-men's gods. If these children were not sent, then the leopard-men would come to the Marti village and take all of the chief's family.

The purpose of the *shauri* was not to decide whether this demand should be ignored, or whether the Marti should take the field and destroy the leopard-men. It was to decide whose children should be sent, and with this I knew that there were leopard-men.

After two hours they had not decided who should be sent, and they looked at me. I stood up, and I mouthed the compliments, the turgid courtesies of all *shauri*, and I spoke of my disgust and shame to find the Marti so cowardly. I had always believed them to be warriors and afraid of nothing. The eyes of the old men flicked over my Lumbwa, who were indeed great warriors and greater than the Marti could ever be, but who were now trembling like women, and I knew my words had no strength with the Marti. I threatened them with punishment. I said that if their children were handed over thus, then the Government would consider them murderers and would hang the old chief in the middle of his village.

The Government was miles away across the grass, and meant nothing to them. The Government was not only miles away, it was centuries away, and could mean nothing to them.

The witch doctors flapped their bones and shook their charms at me, and I became angry with their histrionics, and I asked them what kind of medicine they had if it was useless against these leopard-men. They smiled, they said the magic of the *jablanket-machoies* was stronger.

The old chief was unhappy about my anger, and I think he knew that I would tell the Government, and that sooner or later the askaris would come for him. He believed that if he said he would not send the children to the Amala ford, I would go away, and once I had gone the Marti would send the children. He told me the children would not be sent, but he did not look me in the face, and I knew that he was lying.

I said, "When are the children to be sent to the ford of the Amala?"

He said, "In ten days."

I asked, "What children?"

He said they would be children of poor parents who owned little livestock, but that I was not to worry; now I had come the children would not be sent.

I said, "And if you sent them, how would they go alone on this three-day journey without being killed by lion or buffalo?"

He said the Bwana knew the children would not now be sent, but if they had been sent then two warriors would have gone with them, for that had been in the orders of the leopard-men. The children were to be escorted to the banks of the Amala and left there, but the Bwana must know that this would not happen now, because the Bwana had advised against it. And I understood what he was trying to tell me. He wanted me to know that he was lying, and he hoped that I would be there at the Amala ford and that I would kill the leopard-men for him.

So I told him that I could see into his mind, and these things I would not do. There was a great sadness in his face, but there was still cunning in him, and he stood up and spoke again.

He said that because the Bwana had great magic the children would be given to him, so that he might make up his mind whether to give them to the leopard-

men or not. A great grunt of surprise came from the old
men, but one of the witch doctors vehemently supported the idea, and I could see what was in his mind.
He hoped the leopard-men would kill me, too.

I was sorry for the chief, he had done as much as
he could in face of the threat from the leopard-men
and the risk of the Government's anger. He had placed
all the responsibility on me.

The next morning the four children were brought
to me with great ceremony. They were all about twelve
years old, two boys and two girls, and their parents had
dressed them with great care. I do not know if they
knew what was to happen to them, but they were afraid,
and the girls trembled.

The chief said good-by to me, and what he was
thinking was in his face. He knew that I would not de-
liver these children to the Amala ford, but he was also
wondering what the leopard-men would do when their
sacrifice did not arrive.

I went down the slope, and my Lumbwa followed
me silently, and they too were wondering what I was
going to do. After five miles, with the children trotting
along behind me in silence, I halted. I told the Lumbwa
that we were going to Tamani's village, where I would
ask the Masai chief to lend me a regiment of his *elmorani* to take against the leopard-men and destroy them.
These, I pointed out, would be Loita Masai, not Setick
Lumbwa. My boys listened glumly. They did not like
the Masai, they did not believe the Masai would go
against the leopard-men, but if I did persuade them

then the Lumbwa would lose face before the Masai. Whichever way they looked at the situation, it depressed them.

Tamani, my friend, was very rich, the owner of two thousand cattle, thirty thousand fat-tailed sheep, and half a dozen sleek wives who were the solace of his old age. He had been a great warrior, and he was proud of the courage of his red-haired *elmorani*. I really thought that these lion killers would spit in the dust at the mention of leopard-men.

We arrived in the village at dusk, and there were drums beating and horns blowing, women screaming, and a white, crazy fear in the eyes of the *elmorani*. My Lumbwa looked at this and felt better. Tamani greeted me diffidently, his thoughts on other things. I sat down before him and gave him gifts and asked him what troubled his people.

He said that early in the morning two young *enditos* had gone to gather firewood and had not returned. A party of perhaps ten leopards had been seen carrying the girls over their shoulders, and some of the leopards had run on four legs and some had walked on two, and some had carried guns. All had left the spoor of leopards' pads.

I said, "*Jablanket-machoies?*"

And he said, "It is true Bwana Mkuba."

I asked him why the Loita Masai, whom I knew to be the greatest warriors in the world (which I said softly so that my Lumbwa could not hear) had not pursued and killed these animals.

It was a simple explanation: the leopard-men were neither animals nor men, they were devils and could not be killed.

I said that I had already saved four children of the Marti from the leopard-men. I pointed to them. I said that if Tamani would give me half a regiment of *elmorani* I would destroy the leopard-men and bring back his *endito*. This, I said, he should know and believe, and would know and believe for he was a great man of medicine.

He said sadly that his medicine was as useless as dust before the leopard-men.

That night I saw fires out on the plains about five or six miles away, red blotches against the darkness, and some of the Masai warriors came out of their huts and stared at the fires and murmured unhappily. Before dawn I went to Tamani and told him that I was going to see who had lit these fires, because I believed it to have been the leopard-men. I said I would go alone, if necessary, but that I would be proud to take his *elmorani* with me. I would not only feel proud, but safer, although this I did not tell Tamani.

He looked at me from behind the sleep in his eyes, and he said he would tell his warriors to follow me, but that he did not believe they would follow me very far.

I had fixed the point of the fires in a blanket of trees below a far ridge. My Lumbwa lagged until they were swallowed by the equally reluctant cloud of *elmorani* that Tamani had ordered to follow. When we reached the forest patch, Arab Moina halted. I called to him, but he shook his head, and drove his spear into

the ground, as if marking the spot beyond which he
would not go.

I went into the trees cautiously for half a mile until
I heard voices, the voices of girls talking softly in fear
and in the Masai tongue. I went from tree to tree until
I touched the edge of a glade. I saw the girls first, five
of them, bound to a tree. Two of them were Loita Masai,
and the others were Wanderobo.

There were the gray ash piles of three or four fires,
and stretched about them were perhaps thirty leopards,
but they were not lying as leopards lie when they sleep.
Their bodies were stretched as men stretch in the rest-
less minutes before awakening. I saw black legs, black
arms beneath the skins.

Three more were crouched by the fire, sitting with
legs crossed, gnawing at bones, and these two were men,
although the skins of leopards came up over their backs
and along their arms, with the claws over their fingers,
and the great, fanged heads of the leopard making
hoods.

I pushed back the safety catch of my rifle, and I
stepped into the glade. I called "*Samama!* Stand up!"

The three by the fire sprang up, and one reached
for a musket. I fired and he rolled over in the white ash
of the fire and screamed as it burned him. Now the
others awoke, coming so quickly from sleep that they
looked at me stupidly. They were ugly. The skulls of
leopards fitted tightly to their heads, thrust backward
from their faces, with the teeth jutting down, and they
looked like thirty full-grown leopards rearing up with
open jaws.

I walked over, skirting them, and I cut the thongs that held the girls to the tree. They ran, screaming toward Tamani's village.

I hated the sight of those skins, and I shouted for them to be taken off. The thongs were slipped from wrists and ankles and the skins fell down, and here were rearing leopards no longer but naked men with sullen and frightened faces.

From their tribal markings I knew them to be men of the Washie, and the Ukerrari and the Majama tribes, and I wanted to laugh, for such men were not devils and had not even a tenth of the courage of the Masai.

I asked them why they were masquerading in leopard skins, and they looked sly and said that they poached elephants. In this way they could move unnoticed, which was nonsense, and I knew they were trying to insult me with the explanation, while their eyes went furtively to the edges of the glade.

I said, "Why eat the *endito* of the Masai?"

They were indignant. They said they captured the girls to be their slaves. I did not look at the bones by the fire, and I did not know whether they were speaking the truth, for although I knew that the Majama would eat anything, the Ukerrari I had believed to be fish-eaters.

Now the *elmorani* of the Masai came running up, and with them Arab Moina and my Lumbwa. The girls had passed them and told them what had happened. They came in calling, with their spears raised. The leopard-men ran for the forest and that half a regiment of Masai swung past me proudly in pursuit.

I picked up one of the skins. It was not a complete skin, not, that is, a skin from one leopard, but a cape cunningly tailored from several skins, with the head made into a cap so that the lower jaw fitted below a man's chin with the upper jaw coming down like a visor. Teeth had been reset in the gumless bone.

The feet were ingenious. The leopard-men had made sandals from the pads, filling them with wild rubber.

The Masai took back the skins to Tamani on their bloody spears, and the feasting lasted two days.

Bwana Mkuba and the Memsahib

I met my wife on a Union Castle liner, said Jordan, when I was coming back to Africa one year, and we were married in Mombasa Cathedral. Whatever else happened to that marriage, we started it well by making her the first white woman to cross Africa. I had always wanted to make this crossing, but I had thought of doing it alone, and I don't know why I suggested it to her except that a four-thousand-mile trek across mountain and jungle seemed an original honeymoon. The alternative was to take her on safari, but East Africa then was full of ladies going on safari with their gentlemen, and Eva was woman enough to want to do something different.

It was a long time ago and the details are hazed, but I see the picture of her now and then, against a background of tall elephant grass, or the dark trees of Ituri, very English, very erect on a white muscat donkey, her wide sola topi with its muslin band, her blouse and khaki skirt; or sitting in a Congo canoe among naked boatmen, as calm as if her carriage were taking her to tea with a bishop.

There were six of us altogether when we set off across the Serengati plain, moving northwestward to Lake Victoria, with supplies for a year, with donkeys, porters, guides, dogs, and with great plans for capturing animals which we would sell to European zoos. There were six Europeans in the beginning, including yet another man who was to take moving pictures, but when we reached the east bank of Victoria the others grew cold at the thought of thousands of miles yet unwalked, and they shook hands with us and said good-by in that embarrassed but overhearty way people have when they are ashamed of deserting you, and they left, taking with them half of the three hundred porters I had hired.

That I remember, and remember wondering whether this had weakened Eva's resolve, but she took it calmly, and inferred that you don't take your friends on your honeymoon, even in Africa.

And I remember going down with fever, and coming out of it to find my leg with an abcess on it, as if it still resented the bullet, the spear and the mamba bite. But we went on, and the boys carried me across the Tecoti river in a blanket, while the Memsahib rode her donkey and played the Bwana Mkuba with some skill.

On the last three days to the Congo frontier we rode through England, the parkland at the foot of Mount Ruwenzori, where it pushes its snowhead from a blanket of thick timber. There the air was clean of fever and dirt and sickness, and the land ran down with its orchard-spaced trees to the silver disc of Lake George. We watched the flamingos go up, pink and white and leg-dangling, like a roll of applause. We saw buffalo black on the bluffs, and rock formations like Gothic ruins. And these were fine things to show a woman you had just married, and there was nothing at all to walking across Africa, even though at that moment your leg was smoldering and you were being carried in a blanket.

Katse was the last station on the British frontier, and we came down to it soon after dawn one day. Along the crusted rim of the lake two thousand natives were scooping up salt, and the King of Toro's tax collectors were making sure that His Majesty got his tithe.

We got to Kasindi where it was locked in a dry, yellow, three-sided mountain box, the wind coming in hot even across the lakes, and now and then a storm ripped up the tents and rolled them away along with the blankets and the kettles and the Memsahib's bath, and left me naked for the rain to fall mercifully on a burning leg.

A doctor came over from Beni, where there was a sleeping-sickness station. He came over with his box of knives, and he cut and sliced and let the poison out of me with the best manner in the world. The Belgians asked us where we were going, and we said, "The Atlantic." And they said, "You will never get over the Rukutu; the mountain tribes are spearing whites."

But we went, for over there was the Semiliki valley where I had seen the elephants in their thousands, and this I wanted Eva to see too, for I was showing her my Africa as a man has to show his wife his way of living and his delight in living. The Semiliki ran flat through the valley, widening, narrowing, curving and thrusting, and now and then prettily silvered as it lipped over the stones.

The natives, instead of spearing us, lay by the side of the trail with their throats swollen and their brains addled, dying of sleeping sickness, killed by a tiny, gray-black fly that folds its wings into a quaint swallowtail when it is at rest on your skin and poisoning your blood. Old men and young men, and women and children lay there, perhaps wondering, if their curdled thoughts could wonder anything, why they were dying and we were living. This was no honeymoon for a bride, but it was Africa.

One night—it could have been any night, I do not remember; but a night when that sleeping death was about us for miles—some of the boys ran away, and I could not blame them.

Even the game deserted that saddened world. The grass was empty of buck. The whole land was grieving, and our boys listened each morning for the call of the honey bird and did not hear it. They listened for Ol Toilo and it sang us no luck with our hunting.

We found a village with food, some sweet potatoes in a *shamba* that was protected by thick thornbushes, and guarded further by a hedge of spearmen, as if they could hold sickness at bay with thorns and spears. They would sell us no food. The headman came out and looked at us coldly. His nakedness was discreetly hidden by a red blanket. He wore a head strap of leather, orna-mented with white beads, and there was a stone oint-ment pot bound to his right temple. A string of his children rolled in the dust behind him. He would sell us no food.

The Memsahib, who knew the social decencies on occasions like this, offered him tea. He first passed the cup to his chamberlain, and when the man drank and did not die, then the chief drank too. But it did not soften his face, and his spearmen still guarded the shamba.

The Memsahib had the solution. She called for the phonograph, for this was no Livingstone trek, this had all the comforts then known to civilization, and she had insisted on the phonograph.

It was brought to her, and she got down on her knees and wound it, and the children were quiet, and the chief looked uneasy. She played a record. It was one of those laughing songs, sung by Harry Lauder, a song with belly-moving laughter that made you laugh with it. Soon the chief was laughing, and his chamberlain, and his wives and his children, and the spearmen, rolling on the ground, and this was something Harry Lauder could never have thought he would be able to do.

They sold us some potatoes.

The Memsahib queened it for days, so much so that she went out hunting elephant with a very old Snider, and fortunately never got close enough to elephant to discover how useless that gun could be.

We left the sickness behind us and the land came to life. We were delirious with the ease of the shooting where the cool air came down from the mountain snow,

and the lions coughed about our camp at night. That I
remember well, and I remember the little spearman who
came into camp one dawn and said that he had come
to arrest one of my porters for stealing salt. This had
been a great robbery, for to steal two canoeloads of salt
the man had killed four of his own tribe.

Yet the spearman was so small that I thought my
boy, who was a giant, would break his neck in simple
disgust at the impertinence. But the spearman was the
son of a chief, and my boy surrendered without resent-
ment, and said good-by to us and went off, to be hanged
most probably.

There were no roads, no roads that men had made.
There were the pounded paths of elephant, and then
the timber began to fill up the valley, mimosa and thorn-
bush, and sausage trees with their ridiculous pendant
fruit.

We camped in the ruins of a Catholic Mission, and
there was nothing about it to explain why it had been
abandoned, except that perhaps the sleeping sickness
had been there too. The gardens were full of grenadillas
and pineapples and pomegranates. The Mission stood on
a hill, on an arm of the valley, looking down on the
plain where there were native villages, emptied by the
sickness too, and the wild timothy grass white here
and there with bones.

A white man came into our camp, tall and gaunt,
with that soft, inward-searching expression you see on
the faces of men who have been alone a long time. His
name was Lund, and with two porters he was walking

from the Cape to Cairo, which made him something of a pioneer, too. There are men who are driven to test the endurance of their bodies and their minds, and the way they may choose to do this is unimportant and often foolhardy, but the real truth of what they do is that they must prove themselves able to do it. It was like this with Lund.

But he was going blind, and he knew that he would never see Cairo, even if his porters took him there and did not desert him. He dined with us and he was polite and spoke little of his coming blindness. It gave him great pleasure to see my wife, and he behaved as if he wanted her to know that it was good to see a woman again before this blindness happened.

Even had he not gone blind, he would not have seen Cairo. He got to Lado and there he died, I heard, although what it was that killed him I was not told. It could have been one of many things, for death has a wide range of instruments in Africa.

We went up the Mwambi road, where the hunting was good and the forest built a roof above us and turned the sunlight to green water. This was the place where Stanley gave the world a cliché. This was Darkest Africa, and we cut our way through it with *pangas*.

We were told of a village called Makupees where was buried a great chief in a sarcophagus of ivory. We went through the forest for two hours, and down to a plain where the grass was green and the timber hung on the shoulders of the hills like thickly knitted shawls. No white men had been to this village before, and the women came out in their modest nudity, round-bellied children peering through their legs, all came out to stare at a white woman riding a white donkey.

There was the great chief's grave, a mound of earth with calabashes of decaying food at its foot, rags of bright cloth on spears, and around it a palisade of tusks going up and bending over as if mourning. I counted forty of them before I stopped counting, and all must have weighed over sixty pounds each, but they were old and saffron-colored, and termites had eaten away their roots.

So the valley was good for elephants, and I shot four big bulls in one day, and the Memsahib made a great show of indifference when the boys cut through the abdominal walls and let out the flower of the entrails.

We camped on hilltops and saw dawn before it reached the dark valley bottoms. I saw the forests rolling northward and I wondered what lay in them, and I promised myself that one day I would discover, but it was a promise I never kept.

We went down one river in three dugouts, and here the river traveled quickly in swift waves, swinging away as the palm leaves bent down to snatch at the water. Little, dark men, with wild eyes and curled beards, swung out of the branches and fired arrows at us, and Eva, sitting regally on a chair in the middle of her boatmen, pulled an arrow from the wall of the canoe, and held it up laughing. She asked why it had this sticky glue on the head.

I said that it was poison, and she dropped it calmly in the water.

They buried a chief in the village. We came to it at dusk, landing from the canoes when night joined dark water. There was dancing in the firelight, and a great beating of drums, the braying of horns, as if there were pleasure at the chief's good fortune in slipping from this life.

The villages from Irumi to Stanleyville had been built by Arab slave traders a century, two centuries ago, and they were clean and neat behind thick white walls. The doors were of soft, crimson wood, and as beautifully carved as any you could see in Zanzibar. Some of the villages were wholly Arab communities, and there were silken green flags of Islam on the walls. The men carried muskets with swan's-neck stocks, bound with silver, and had gold-hilted daggers in their sashes. Their faces were dignified and proud, and they looked so much like warriors that you could be forgiven for not recognizing them as traders.

The old Arab chief came down to greet us, and his slaves came behind him, carrying poultry and eggs and fruit, and rice for our porters. He took tea with us, and smiled out of his wrinkled face to my wife.

I spoke to him in Kiswhalli which made him happy enough to chuckle at every word, and he was pleased that I should wish to talk of the slave trade, for it was on this ranging commerce that his people had built an empire when his grandfather had been a child.

He remembered Tip-o-Tee, he said, and this man had been the greatest Arab slave raider of all the centuries. His canoes had traveled from the mouth of the Congo to its rise. His caravans had been protected by clouds of cavalry. Tip-o-Tee had been a great man and cunning, for when he realized that the tribes of Ujiji country were cunning and adaptable, he did not take them as slaves, but organized them under chiefs of his own appointing and made them raiders too. Tip-o-Tee took slaves that were shipped to the Persian gulf and the Americas.

The people of Ujiji learned well and admired the Arabs, and when slavery was abolished and the Arabs accepted this, the Ujiji people continued raiding on their own, and hired out their slaves as porters.

They raided still, said the old man, and chuckled. He said that sometimes at night, when the forests were quiet, you could hear the guns and the cries in the far distance.

She shot a lion.

I had wounded him and he went into the scrub, and I told her to go back to camp, but she smiled and waited until I had given her all the reasons why a wounded lion should not be followed by a woman, and then she smiled again and said, "Shall we go?"

We put the dogs on leash and went after the lion. We followed the trackers as they picked a grass blade, a stone, and held them up to show that the blood-spoor was still being made. We found where the lion had rejoined the pride and rested with it in the grass.

Then, half a mile from a stream, the wounded one had turned and left the others, and I knew that it must be badly hit, and all the more dangerous because of it. The trackers went up to thick bush, and came back saying they could smell the scent of lion there.

We released the dogs and they went in, with Ginger leading. The lion roared, and I looked at Eva and saw her mouth tighten, but she need not have been ashamed of this, for I never liked the sound. The dogs teased the lion until it came out. It came out slowly. We could see the head, the black mane, the slap of its paw as it hit a dog.

Then it came out of the bush and saw us and roared. It was very close.

Eva put her sporting .303 to her shoulder, and I said that she was to hold it on the lion's chest and not think of this as a lion. When she fired I fired too, and I do not know which of us hit it, but it went down quickly and met the ground with a thump, and I knew that the bullet had found the heart. The boys ran up and put their fingers in the hole gravely, and said, "*Piga*, Memsahib!" very proud of her.

She was proud too, and she had the right to be. Even if it was my shot, she had still faced a wounded lion.

She was not well, and we knew that the middle of Africa was no place for a white woman to have a child. We left Avukubi with the boys carrying her in a chair, and they laughed and they sang as they carried her, for they knew. We marched at moonrise, because it was cool at night, pitching tent at four in the morning, with dawn coming out of the rain behind us.

We found a white man on the trail and he was alone, and ill with fever, with his eyes sunk in his head. I dosed him with quinine and we left him some soup, and he said his boys would be coming for him soon. I wondered. I still wonder if they did come, or whether he died there of fever by the trail. I have forgotten his name, or why he was there, or what he was doing, or whether he was English, French or Belgian, just that he lay by the roadside burning with fever, but conscious enough to thank me for the quinine and say that it was all right, his boys would be along soon, like a man refusing a lift in your car because a bus would be along soon.

Then we climbed out of the heat and the wet forest, and the blood came back to her cheeks. The trees lay below us in an immobile green pool. The hills went up to the wind and beyond them lay Stanleyville on the arc of the Congo.

She got out of her chair and said she would walk, because now the boys were too weak to carry her. I had no strength to argue with her because there was pain in my shoulder from the time we had been thrown from the canoe into the Semiliki. The boys marched sullenly now, without singing.

We got down a valley wall to a little mud town called Gorma, and there Eva said thank you, but did I mind, she could go no further. Then she lay down in the tent and said nothing. I got a boy and I put him on my Arab and told him he could kill the horse if he had to, but he was to bring a doctor from Stanleyville. He did kill the Arab, but he brought a doctor.

And the doctor came too late. An old chief's wife from Bufwaboli came over, and she was wise in these things, yet even her wisdom was useless. I helped her, but this was something I knew nothing about, and I let her tell me.

When the doctor arrived, the child had been born. It was born dead. It was a girl, the old woman said.

I bought a chimpanzee from a Frenchman in Bufwaboli, because I thought it would amuse her as she was carried along in the hammock, but this was the only bad chimpanzee I ever had. There was a devil inside of it, and it frightened her.

Now the fever hit me again, and we made slow time to Stanleyville. There was a road of sorts, a road which a white man was making to his home thirty miles outside Stanleyville, and hundreds of native road makers lay by the side of it, smoking, and sleeping in the rain.

She grew well at Stanleyville and we did not speak of what had happened at Gorma. I lay ill with fever and prickly heat, and the sisters from the hospital came across the river in their white habits and insisted on taking me back. The Italian doctor looked at me and said he was happy I had come to him, because after one encounter with our chimpanzee, he had decided not to come to me again.

Now all we had to do was go down the great river

to its mouth, and what pain and struggle there was in crossing Africa was behind us. I was tempted to stay at La Romeo, the land was good, and the hunting was good, but Eva wanted to go home to England, and this I could not refuse her.

We went down to Kinchassa on a stern-wheeler, and we listened to the drums talking to the ship all the way down. All day and all night the drums beat, and we lay beneath awnings on the deck and listened to them, and to the rustle of the great wheels. We watched the crew feeding logs to the fires, and the river went past us, green, cream, black and red, day after day. The crocodile slept on islands in the sun, the thick papyrus grass grew out into the water and onto the mud flats and snatched at us. We enjoyed the splendid beauty of the native in the bows, calling the fathoms as he tested the water with a bamboo pool. We listened to the bell in the engine room. We listened to the sad night calls of Africa from bank to bank, and I was ashamed of myself for traveling across Africa in this indolent fashion.

We came back to West Africa for I had decided to take a concession of fifty-five thousand acres near Thysville, and although I did not know it, my days in Africa as a lonely hunter were over. It was good land, that concession, high, where the air was fresh, and it was part of my contract that I should keep at least a thousand head of cattle. I built a house of wattle and daub for Eva and myself, with a veranda looking down on the open plains and the green patches of forest. I built roads, and bridges, and saw pits. I planted a vegetable garden, and these were strange things for an ivory poacher to be doing, and when the strangeness of it struck me, I went out and hunted elephant. It was in those days that I saw the King Elephant, and perhaps my failure to kill him was symbolic.

Nothing came of my concession, because the Kaiser's war began, and we went home.

We came back to Thysville after the war, but my concession had lapsed. Who could keep a thousand head of cattle and still be away four years in a war?

You couldn't get a boat direct to the Belgian Congo in those days, and we went to the Cape. I knew our only chance was to go up part of the way by cargo boat and then trek through the interior. I bought horses, wagons, yokes and twenty oxen. We swam our oxen ashore at Loanda and broke them there to the yoke, and we were laughed at when we began the trek. The country was dry and waterless. My boys deserted. The cattle died with lung sickness, and we abandoned them, the wagons, and the equipment, and went on to Bembe alone on horseback.

I became a planter again, at Luvu between San Salvador and the Congo. I became a planter and I planted cotton, coffee, ginger, pepper and avenues of oranges, lemons and limes. And perhaps I did not realize the change that had come over me. It was more than twenty years since I had come up from Port Elizabeth to prospect for gold, to become a hunter who hated towns, who hated houses, who was content alone in the forest.

I found outcrops of silver and copper, and I found a stream where the bed was strewn with thousands of meteorites that were almost pure nickel. The old excitement passed into me, and passed out of me, when I discovered that an American company had the blanket rights of all minerals in that area.

Eva became ill again, with some undefined but persistent poisoning. Whatever Africa meant to me, or had meant to me, it was not her country.

I sent her down to the Baptist Mission at San Salvador, sixty miles away, where there was a doctor and a hospital. I sent nearly all my boys with her so that the journey could be done in one day. They had been gone a week, and I was alone in the house with a gale pressing down the forest outside and lifting the roof and banging it down on the piles, when a native came out of the darkness, holding a note wrapped in oilskin, stuck in a cleft stick.

The doctor wrote that Eva was ill with blackwater.

I saddled Baby, my South African mare. I put a rifle under my thigh and hung a hurricane lamp from the saddle horn. I had seen storms in Africa when the land seemed to heave upward to meet the lightning, but this was the most terrible I had ever seen. Before me the trees seemed to move and sway, like soft reeds below the surface of running water. We came to rivers where the bridges were down, and I swam Baby across, holding her tail. For miles I led her, pulling her bridle as she shied from the lightning with her hoofs up.

It took me twelve hours to reach the Mission, and
the storm had gone when I got there, so too had the
climax of the fever.

But Eva could not stay in Africa. She went home,
but I stayed.

I stayed a year, two years. I went home and came
back. I was older. When I had been young I had taken
pride in the tusker I could bring down with one shot,
not in the thought of groves of orange trees which now
gave me happiness. Yet what was happening to me was
happening to Africa. The years of the hunters were passing, gone in the war, and this was the land of the settler.

The hunter makes a poor settler. The Portuguese
Government raised the hut tax, and my entire labor
force deserted me. The forest flowed back over my plantations, choked the life out of my orange groves.

I went hunting in a desperate swan song, and, as
if she were angry at my thoughts of leaving her, Africa
turned her ugly side to me as a valediction. In something
very close to a mood of madness I went after a chimera,
a weird, strange animal which the natives said could be
found in the forest along the Ponso River. Perhaps I did
not believe in this animal, or perhaps I did; or perhaps
I wanted to snatch one last secret out of the continent.

We trekked north beneath soft skies, through winds
with health in them. The moon at night was luminous
and the trees were silver-leafed. But in a day or two days
we reached a forest where vines hung from tree to tree
and fought the trees for the air and for the sunlight.
Great fungi as tall as a man grew sickly white in the

darkness, and as each plant grew it crushed beneath it that which had grown earlier, until the air stank with death and decay.

Water, where we found it, was black and green, oily whirlpools sucking it down into the earth. I went no more than a mile into this forest before I knew I could go no further. I went back and sat on its edge and listened to its silence.

There Africa played a last little act of cruelty for me. I was watching a thick, yellow-green vine swaying gently, when a leopard padded softly beneath it, lips back in a snarl, for it had scented me. It paused beneath the vine with paw upraised, and then the vine dropped lazily and held it in a coil, wrapping another coil about it, and another, until the leopard stopped snarling and clawing, and the python had crushed it. I killed the python.

At Thysville the doctor put away his stethoscope and his thermometer, and smiled at me. The sun came pleasantly through the slats of the windows. The walls were white, and the floor polished.

I was rotten with malaria, he said. If I stayed another year in Africa, it would kill me. If the malaria did not kill me, which it would, there was that leg that had taken the bullet, the spear and the bite. There was the shoulder which my Lumbwa had wrenched back into place. There were many other things about me that made him uneasy. How long did I think a man's heart could stand the strain I had put on mine over twenty years?

I should go to a cold climate and get the fever out of my system.

"Oregon?" I said, thinking of my grandfather.

"It will do," he said, "but don't come back to Africa."

I sold Baby to the Catholic Mission. I sold my dogs to Government officials. I passed Pete, my Swazi boy, the only one who had not deserted us on the trek up from Loanda, over to the British Consul. I sold all my equipment except a .500 Express, and I was to lose that later in Antwerp. I took nothing into Africa, and I brought nothing out.

I had another bout of malaria, and this I sweated out alone in my room in the Queen's Hotel. When I came out of it, I was ready to go home. If home was what I could call a country I had ignored for twenty-five years.

The Little Brown Honey Bird Again

That's it, said Jordan, not all of it, but some of it that I can still remember. I am seventy-five and these things began over half a century ago. When I look out of the window, here in Berkshire, I can see a long rampart of green turf, higher than a man and with sloping banks. You see it, where the children are playing with a ball? It is said to have been a Roman earthwork, and if it was, then it is more than fifteen hundred years old, so what are my seventy-five?

The earth is all that endures, and an ordinary man survives only by what mark he leaves on it. I left no mark on Africa, none that you could find, for the tractor and the automobile have passed over the ground where my fires burned and my *bomas* were built. The forests have taken back my plantations. But my Africa was a frontier and what I did there, what was done by Selous and John Boyes, by Will Judd and Banks and Pearson, men like these, had to be done before the settlers could come, and the road makers and the railway builders. I believe that an untamed land must test the strength of man before it is willing to surrender. Not that I saw myself as a trail maker. I chose to live the way I did because I liked it, because it called for strength and gave me strength, and this is what a man enjoys in living. Perhaps it was right that when I turned and tried to become a settler myself, saw myself as a land owner, perhaps it was right that my body should refuse the change and make it impossible for me to stay in Africa without dying.

If I regret the passing of my Africa it is a peculiar and personal regret, and one that does not make me bitter. It is the way you are sorry that you can no longer do the things you did in your youth. Africa is still a rich land, and the richness is no longer remote, something only a lone elephant hunter can find and enjoy. Its richness is in the promise of its earth, as it always was. That much I knew even as I hunted across it. There were times when I could see the farms and the herds and the roads and mines and towns that were to come, and my happiness lay in seeing the land before these things came. I am as vain as any man, and my vanity was perhaps something like Lund's. I enjoyed being first on the ground. I enjoyed the knowledge that it took courage and skill to be first on the ground.

It is many years since I heard the song of the little brown honey bird. Once I could imitate it, but now I have lost the trick of that. I have not forgotten his invitation. He is still there, singing for any who wish to hear him.

Printed in the United Kingdom
by Lightning Source UK Ltd.
9843400001B/225